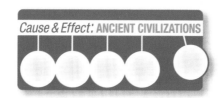

Cause & Effect: ANCIENT CIVILIZATIONS

Cause & Effect:
The Ancient Aztecs

Don Nardo

ReferencePoint
Press®

San Diego, CA

© 2018 ReferencePoint Press, Inc.
Printed in the United States

For more information, contact:
ReferencePoint Press, Inc.
PO Box 27779
San Diego, CA 92198
www.ReferencePointPress.com

LIBRARY OF CONGRESS CATALOGING-IN-PUBLICATION DATA

Name: Nardo, Don, 1947- author.
Title: Cause & Effect: The Ancient Aztecs/by Don Nardo.
Other titles: Ancient Aztecs
Description: San Diego, CA : ReferencePoint Press, Inc., 2017. | Series:
   Cause & Effect: Ancient Aztecs| Includes bibliographical
   references and index.| Audience: Grade 9-12.
Identifiers: LCCN 2017002449 (print) | LCCN 2017010590 (ebook) | ISBN
   9781682821466 (hardback) | ISBN 9781682821473 (eBook)
Subjects: LCSH: Aztecs.
Classification: LCC F1219.73 .N373 2017 (print) | LCC F1219.73 (ebook) | DDC
   972--dc23
LC record available at https://lccn.loc.gov/2017002449

CONTENTS

"History is a complex study of the many causes that have influenced happenings of the past and the complicated effects of those varied causes."

—William & Mary School of Education,
Center for Gifted Education

Understanding the causes and effects of historical events and time periods is rarely simple. The largest and most influential empire of ancient India, for instance, came into existence largely because of a series of events set in motion by Persian and Greek invaders. Although the Mauryan Empire was both wealthy and well organized and benefited enormously from strong rulers and administrators, the disarray sowed by invading forces created an opening for one of India's most ambitious and successful ancient rulers—Chandragupta, the man who later came to be known in the West as the "Indian Julius Caesar." Had conditions in India at the time been different, the outcome might have been something else altogether.

The value of analyzing cause and effect in the context of ancient civilizations, therefore, is not necessarily to identify a single cause for a singular event. The real value lies in gaining a greater understanding of that civilization as a whole and being able to recognize the many factors that gave shape and direction to its rise, its development, its fall, and its lasting importance. As outlined by the National Center for History in the Schools at the University of California–Los Angeles, these factors include "the importance of the individual in history . . . the influence of ideas, human interests, and beliefs; and . . . the role of chance, the accidental and the irrational."

ReferencePoint's Cause & Effect: Ancient Civilizations series examines some of the world's most interesting and important civilizations by focusing on various causes and consequences. For instance, in *Cause & Effect: Ancient India*, a chapter explores how one Indian ruler helped transform Buddhism into a world religion. And in *Cause & Effect: Ancient Egypt*, one chapter delves into the importance of the Nile River in the development of Egyptian civilization. Every book in the series includes thoughtful discussion of questions like these—supported by facts, examples, and a mix of fully documented primary and secondary source quotes. Each title also includes an overview of the civilization so that readers have a broad context for understanding the more detailed discussions of causes and their effects.

The value of such study is not limited to the classroom; it can also be applied to many areas of contemporary life. The ability to analyze and interpret history's causes and consequences is a form of critical thinking. Critical thinking is crucial in many professions, ranging from law enforcement to science. Critical thinking is also essential for developing an educated citizenry that fully understands the rights and obligations of living in a free society. The ability to sift through and analyze complex processes and events and identify their possible outcomes enables people in that society to make important decisions.

The Cause & Effect: Ancient Civilizations series has two primary goals. One is to help students think more critically about the human societies that once populated our world and develop a true understanding of their complexities. The other is to help build a foundation for those students to become fully participating members of the society in which they live.

IMPORTANT EVENTS IN THE HISTORY OF THE ANCIENT AZTECS

ca. CE 1122
The Aztecs believed they began their great migration from their original homeland into the Valley of Mexico on this date.

1325
The Aztecs begin erecting their capital city of Tenochtitlán on islands in Lake Texcoco.

ca. CE 900
The Toltecs, an inventive Mesoamerican people whom the Aztecs will come to idolize, prosper.

BCE 300 / CE 900   1100   1300

ca. BCE 300
Work begins on the world's largest pyramid at Cholula, which will eventually become part of the extensive Aztec Empire.

ca. 1299
The migrating Aztecs reach the eastern shore of Lake Texcoco.

1428
The Aztecs and their allies defeat the Tepanec people, who had long dominated Mexico's lakes region.

1446
The Aztecs and their neighbors begin to experience a series of devastating natural disasters.

1484
Hernán Cortés, who will one day conquer the Aztecs, is born in Spain.

1535
Spanish priests burn thousands of Aztec books in a huge bonfire.

1502
Montezuma II, who is destined to eventually confront the Spaniards, assumes the Aztec throne.

1520
More than six hundred Spaniards are slain by Aztec warriors on a stone causeway leading out of Tenochtitlán.

1500   1510   1520   1525

1487
The Aztecs sacrifice some eighty thousand war prisoners to their war god.

1521
After a long siege, Cortés and his forces capture Tenochtitlán.

1519
Cortés's expedition leaves Cuba in February bound for the then-mysterious land of Mexico. In April the Spaniards land on Mexico's eastern coast. By September Cortés and his followers reach Tlaxcala, whose residents are enemies of the Aztecs. On November 8 the Spanish forces arrive in Tenochtitlán. On November 16 Cortés orders King Montezuma's arrest.

The Heart of a Toltec

The Aztecs were a Mesoamerican (early Central American) people who appeared in Mexico during the 1200s CE. They dominated the region militarily, politically, and culturally from the early 1400s to early 1500s, when they were conquered by invading Spaniards. In addition to their military exploits, the Aztecs were great builders who also ran successful large-scale farms and produced impressive art and literature.

The Aztecs were also religiously devout, and the beliefs and rituals of their faith were central to their everyday lives. They felt that their gods, although invisible, were always present and watching and judging humans. Another core belief was that those deities ordained certain specific fates for both individuals and entire peoples, and at times they manipulated history to achieve a desired destiny.

The Inventors of Civilization?

One of the most important examples of how those gods created such a destiny was the way in which they supposedly brought about the conditions for the Aztecs' rise to greatness. Relating to that event, it was common for members of Aztec society to use the adage "*Toltecayotl*," meaning "to have a Toltec heart." To the Aztecs, having a Toltec heart meant being a superior individual who excelled at nearly all things.

Clearly, the Aztecs held the Toltecs—a Mesoamerican people who flourished in central Mexico between about 900 and 1170 CE—in the highest esteem. The general belief was that the Toltecs had invented most aspects of civilization. The Aztecs and other inhabitants of precontact Mexico (meaning before white Europeans arrived there) thought their own society made up the entire human race. They did not realize that other peoples existed beyond the two oceans that formed Mexico's eastern and western boundaries.

Also, it was thought that the Toltecs had directly preceded the Aztecs in the region. Central to the Aztecs' beliefs about their own

8

past was the notion that the gods brought about the fall of the once great Toltecs to clear the way for the ascendance of the Aztecs, who thereafter also achieved greatness.

A related belief among the Aztecs was that they were distantly related to and had descended from the Toltecs. Where that idea, now known to be incorrect, came from is unknown. Some modern scholars have suggested that it may have been an example of wishful thinking. The Aztecs were fascinated by the abandoned Toltec city of Tollan (now called Tula), situated roughly 50 miles (80 km) north of what is now Mexico City. To the Aztecs, Tollan was "a fantastic city of mythical proportions and qualities,"[1] as noted historical writer Michael E. Smith puts it. It is not surprising, therefore, that parties of Aztec religious pilgrims made annual journeys from their homeland to Tollan to pray and see for themselves what they thought was the world's first

This modern painting accurately captures the hustle and bustle of an open-air marketplace in the Aztec capital of Tenochtitlán at its height, shortly before the brutal Spanish invasion began.

great city. The desire to believe that they were direct offspring of the inventors of civilization may simply have been too hard for the Aztecs to resist.

The Demise of the Toltecs

Despite the Aztecs' wishful thinking, modern experts have determined that the Aztecs were *not* direct descendants of the Toltecs. Evidence shows that the Aztecs originated far to the north of the central Mexican territory the Toltecs inhabited. Still, that reality does not negate the Aztecs' strongly held belief that the gods had eliminated the Toltecs to make way for the Aztecs.

That belief was based in part on one of the principal Aztec myths about the Toltecs. In the story, the monstrous god of war, Tezcatlipoca, disguised himself as a lowly laborer and entered the Toltec capital, Tollan. Soon he managed to find work as a servant in the royal palace, where he acquired periodic access to the king's daughter. Over time the god subtly and deviously employed his divine powers to make her fall in love with him.

Learning of the princess's feelings for the lower-class stranger, the king became worried that she might agree to marry him. Many common Toltecs heard about what was happening, and out of respect for the royal daughter, they sided with their monarch. Few were surprised, therefore, when the king did his best to rid society of the man who had managed to capture the princess's heart. The ruler ordered the stranger to join the army ranks and to fight in the front line in an upcoming battle with enemy forces. Most Toltecs assumed the newcomer would be killed in short order.

When the two armies met on the battlefield, however, Tezcatlipoca, still in disguise, used his godly strength to easily slay dozens of enemy soldiers. In this way, he instantly became a national hero. Now that everyone had come to admire and trust him, the sneaky divinity executed the final stage of a dastardly plan he had hatched well before. He claimed he would celebrate his new heroic status by holding a huge feast for all of Tollan's residents. "Great crowds assembled," one modern scholar writes, and Tezcatlipoca persuaded everyone to sing and dance. "Faster and faster the people danced, until the pace became so furious that they were driven to madness, lost their footing, and tumbled pell-mell down a deep ravine, where they were changed into rocks."[2]

According to Mesoamerican mythology, after Tezcatlipoca had wiped out the Toltecs, the way was clear for the worthy Aztecs to rise to greatness. The Aztecs assumed this story was true, partly because they did not know the real reasons for the demise of the Toltecs. Historians still debate those reasons, but the scholarly consensus is that there was no single cause of their decline. Famines, rebellions, civil wars, and foreign invasions all took a toll until the few remaining Toltecs abandoned Tollan and dispersed into villages in the countryside.

In whatever manner the Toltecs disappeared from history, more certain is the awe and gratitude the Aztecs felt for them. As researcher Mark Cartwright points out, the latter "seem to have copied many aspects of Toltec religious practices and art and looked on the Toltec period as a golden era when such wonders as writing, medicine, and metallurgy were invented." This explains why "for the Aztecs it was the Toltecs and no other that they sought to claim descent from."[3]

> "[The Aztecs] looked on the Toltec period as a golden era when such wonders as writing, medicine, and metallurgy were invented."[3]
>
> —Researcher Mark Cartwright

CHAPTER ONE

A Brief History of Aztec Civilization

When a small army of Spaniards and other Europeans led by Hernán Cortés arrived in central Mexico in 1519, they were shocked by what they found. They had expected to encounter scattered, tiny villages inhabited by disorganized, primitive, illiterate natives. Instead, they beheld a thriving, sophisticated civilization with a complex social structure, literature, arts, and cities that rivaled the largest and finest in Europe.

The Spaniards noted that numerous and diverse native groups, speaking many different languages, inhabited the region. But nearly all lived under the political and military control of one distinctive people who had carved out a powerful empire containing millions of subjects. California State University anthropologist Frances Berdan describes them as "skillful and tireless, keen and modest. Ferocious in battle and stoic in sacrifice. Builders of magnificent cities and composers of sensitive songs and poems. Who were these people—so clever in both war and poetry? They called themselves Mexica (me-SHEE-ka), although it has become popular today to refer to them as Aztecs."[4]

From an Old to a New Homeland

Unlike many of the peoples native to central Mexico, the Aztecs did not originate there. Rather, they came from somewhere far to the north of the large highland plateau known as the Valley of Mexico, which became the hub of their empire. In their mythological lore, they underwent a migration from a land they called Aztlan. "If Aztlan represents a place grounded in any objective historical reality," says researcher Duncan Ryan, "its location was probably either in what is today the northern regions of Mexico or possibly in the extreme southwest of the United States."[5]

The exact reasons why the Aztec left their original homeland are as mysterious as the location of that legendary place. There is no doubt, however, that sometime during the 1100s CE they slowly but steadily wandered southward toward the Valley of Mexico. Perhaps once they arrived there, the tribe would have passed through and continued its journey had it not been for that region's unique and extremely inviting features.

First, the valley's center was dominated by a complex network of large lakes. These waterways "favored the human populations residing along their shores and on their islands," Berdan explains. "The lakes provided an effective means of transportation" and "were laden with canoe traffic." This invited "commerce and other forms of interaction throughout the valley. The lakes also supplied varied and abundant aquatic resources: fish and fowl, reptile and amphibian." Meanwhile, "a highly productive form of agriculture was practiced in several [nearby] districts by claiming land from the lakes." The well-organized peoples who already lived in the area "produced abundant harvests of a variety of crops."[6] Those foodstuffs were sold in local markets and traded with peoples living both inside and outside the valley.

Believing they had found a suitable new homeland to replace their old one, the Aztecs settled in the valley's central lakes region. Evidence suggests that at first they were viewed as unwelcome outsiders and endured a certain amount of harassment. This forced them to move from time to time to various locales bordering the lakes. Eventually, however, in about 1325, they established a settlement on an island in Lake Texcoco. That small town would in time become the splendid Aztec capital of Tenochtitlán. According to historian Brian M. Fagan, "A more unprepossessing [unattractive] location for a future capital city it would be hard to imagine. Initially, Tenochtitlan was little more than a hamlet on a swampy island at the southern end of Lake Texcoco, the lake that once filled much of the Valley of Mexico. But the Aztecs were nothing if not tough and resourceful."[7]

"The Aztecs were nothing if not tough and resourceful."[7]

—Historian Brian M. Fagan

An Ever-Expanding Economy

In fact, the Aztecs' success as a people, and eventually as avid imperialists who conquered and ruled others, was in many ways due to that toughness. It was characterized by a no-nonsense, diligent approach to hard work and life in general. They also demonstrated that they were versatile and able to swiftly adjust to new conditions and situations.

A good example of the Aztecs' application of these positive qualities when facing a challenge was their success in large-scale agriculture, which formed the base of their booming economy. They did not invent most of the farming methods they employed. Most of these had been in use for centuries by other Mesoamerican peoples who inhabited central Mexico. Part of what made the Aztecs stand out in this area was their leaders' skill in organizing workers to complete big projects. Also, as a people the Aztecs had a very strong work ethic, to use a modern term.

In addition, the Aztecs were also creative farmers. From the early fourteenth century on, they made huge raised gardens known as *chinampas*. Most often those wide swaths of fertile soil were located atop former swamplands. "A layer of mud was spread over part of the chinampa and allowed to harden until it could be cut up into rectangular blocks," states scholar Warwick Bray.

> Then the gardener poked a hole in each block, dropped in a seed, and covered it with manure [made of] human dung which was collected from the city latrines for sale to the farmers. The seedlings were watered in dry weather and protected against sudden frosts. Then at the appropriate time they were transplanted to the main beds and mulched with vegetation cut from the swamps.[8]

In addition, Aztec farmers planted crops in large fields situated along and near the shores of the region's many lakes. As might be expected, these farms, combined with the thousands of *chinampas*, produced an immense and stable food supply not only for Tenochtitlán but also for markets throughout the region. The reliable availability of food contributed to population increases throughout central Mexico.

An illustration from a sixteenth-century Mexican manuscript shows Aztec farmers tending to their crops, grown in *chinampas*, large raised gardens created atop former unusable swamplands.

Evidence suggests that during the late 1300s Tenochtitlán had five times as many residents as it had had when it was founded some seven decades earlier.

The Rise of the Triple Alliance

The political authority of the Aztec capital increased a bit more slowly than its economy. Initially, both the town and its army were small and no match for the larger cities and considerable military forces of some more established peoples in the region. Probably the most formidable of these groups were the Tepanecs. They inhabited Lake Texcoco's western shores. Another strong local group, the Acolhua, dwelled along the enormous lake's eastern shores.

In addition to growing a tremendous number of crops in raised gardens (*chinampas*) and farmers' fields, the Aztecs hunted large numbers of birds, rabbits, deer, and other game. That abundance of food flooded into mammoth outdoor markets throughout the Aztec realm. When the Spaniards first saw these markets, they were stunned by their size and the variety of their goods. One of Cortés's soldiers, Bernal Díaz del Castillo, left behind a description of just one of these markets. It reads in part:

> Let us begin with the dealers in gold, silver, and precious stones, feathers, cloaks, and embroidered goods, and male and female slaves who are also sold there. Some are brought there attached to long poles by means of collars around their necks to prevent them from escaping, but others are left loose. [Next] there were those who sold coarser cloth, and cotton goods and fabrics made of twisted thread, and there were chocolate merchants with their chocolate. In this way you could see every kind of merchandise to be found anywhere in New Spain [Mexico]. [In addition] there were those who sold sisal cloth and ropes and sandals they wore on their feet, which are made from the same plant. All three were kept in one part of the market, in the place assigned to them, and in another part were the skins of tigers and lions [probably jaguars and pumas], otters, jackals, and deer, badgers, mountain cats and other wild animals, some tanned and some untanned, and other classes of merchandise.

Bernal Díaz del Castillo, *The Conquest of New Spain*, trans. J.M. Cohen. New York: Penguin, 1963, p. 232.

For an undetermined number of decades, out of what they saw as necessity, the Aztec kings bowed to the political dominance of the Tepanecs. To acknowledge that supremacy, the Aztecs regularly paid the Tepanec rulers tribute in the form of money or goods meant to express one's submission to a stronger party. Sometimes the Tepanecs demanded that the tribute take the form of young Aztec men to serve in the Tepanec army.

When Aztec men did serve as soldiers, whether for the Tepanecs or the Aztec kings, they gained reputations as excellent fighters. Partly for that reason, as the Aztec nation became larger and more populous and its army grew bigger, its ability to defend itself increased as well. During the 1420s the Aztec king Itzcoatal felt confident enough to openly challenge the Tepanecs. At one point the Tepanec monarch significantly increased the amount of tribute he expected the Aztecs to contribute, and Itzcoatal refused to pay anything at all. Instead, he convinced the rulers of some other Mesoamerican peoples to join him in opposing Tepanec political supremacy. In 1428 a coalition consisting of four groups—the Aztecs, Acolhua, Tlacopan, and Huexotzinco— met the Tepanec army in battle and scored a stunning victory over it.

Thereafter, the Huexotzinco went back to their homeland just outside the Valley of Mexico. The Acolhua and Tlacopan, meanwhile, who lived inside the valley, accepted King Itzcoatal's offer to create a new partnership that would provide mutual protection against outside aggressors. Because three separate nations were involved, it became known as the Triple Alliance.

Each member of the coalition agreed to refrain from going to war with the other two, as well as to continue to support a member when it launched conquests of other peoples. After those peoples had been defeated, any tribute they paid had to be divided equally among the three members. This naturally created a situation in which the three nations developed a policy of regular conquest in order to amass as much tribute as possible. Indeed, Fagan calls the realm controlled by the Triple Alliance a "tribute machine." The Aztecs and their partners "orchestrated campaigns of taxation" and "veiled threats of armed force," he writes. The tribute took a number of forms, among them firewood, "gold dust for fine ornaments, tropical bird feathers for ceremonial headdresses and warriors' uniforms, cotton mantles, tree gum, and animal skins."[9]

The Methods of Maintaining Power

The empire carved out by the Triple Alliance continued to expand in the years following King Itzcoatal's reign. Succeeding Aztec monarchs persisted in using their efficient and feared military as a tool to spread and maintain their influence. Yet they employed diplomatic means as well to achieve that goal. One of the chief examples of this more peaceful approach to foreign policy was maintaining alliances through intermarriage with royal families in other Mesoamerican nation-states. "Marriage alliances," Michael E. Smith points out, "were an important component of diplomacy among Mesoamerican states. Lower ranking kings would endeavor to marry the daughters of more powerful and important kings. A marriage established at least an informal alliance between the polities [nations] and was a public acknowledgement of the dominant status of the more powerful king."[10]

> "Marriage alliances were an important component of diplomacy among Mesoamerican states."[10]
>
> —Scholar Michael E. Smith

The degree to which the Aztecs balanced warfare with diplomacy to further their goals depended on the whims of their king at any given time. There is no doubt that King Montezuma I, who ruled the Aztec realm for twenty-eight years during the mid-1400s, used conquest as his chief tool. His armies defeated peoples who dwelled far beyond the borders of the Valley of Mexico. In this way, most of Mesoamerica became subject to the control of the Triple Alliance and had to pay its leaders tribute.

Another of Montezuma's noteworthy achievements was to initiate construction of the so-called Great Temple, or Templo Mayor, in Tenochtitlán. The structure—a giant pyramid with dual staircases leading to separate shrines for two major gods—became a centerpiece of both the capital city and the Aztec realm in general. The sacrifices the nation's leading priests performed there were thought to maintain state power by making sure the gods remained always on the side of the Aztecs.

This function of the temple became particularly important in the period from 1446 to 1453, when the Aztecs and their neighbors endured a series of devastating natural disasters. These included floods, droughts, and early frosts that destroyed crops and led to starvation in some areas. In part because the peoples of the region were religiously devout, they attributed these calamities to the wrath of one or more gods. It was thought, therefore, that large-scale human sacrifices were necessary to persuade the deities to stop punishing humanity.

Several of these bloody ceremonies were performed after an awful drought in 1453, and not long afterward there was a period of heavy rains that brought abundant crops. Not surprisingly, the Aztecs were now convinced that their rituals had appeased the gods. Thereafter, to ensure those divinities would remain satisfied, the government ordered the state priests to perform regular human sacrifices at the Great Temple and other shrines. Some evidence indicates that in 1487 more than eighty thousand prisoners of war met grisly fates in this manner in Tenochtitlán.

A modern watercolor effectively depicts the great double temple in Tenochtitlán dedicated to the gods Huitzilopochtli and Tlaloc. The cutaway portion shows that the structure was erected atop an earlier temple.

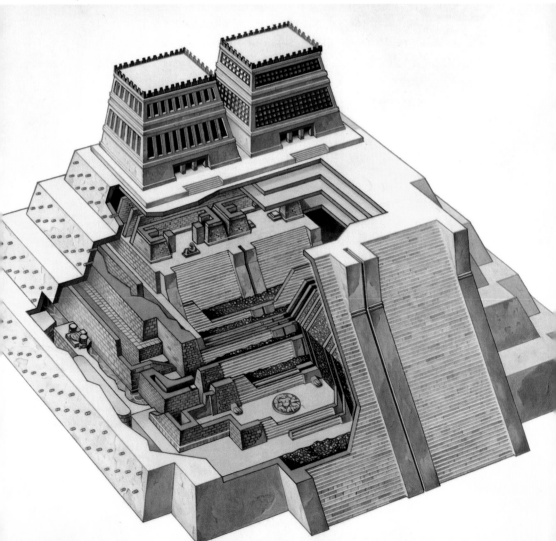

The Aztecs at their Zenith

The Aztec king who presided over that display of ritualistic carnage was Ahuitzotl, who had ascended the throne the year before. His reign was significant for another milestone in the history of the Aztecs, namely their emergence as the imperial masters of Mesoamerica. For a number of years before he came to power the Aztecs were widely recognized as the dominant member of the Triple Alliance. Ahuitzotl simply dropped the pretense that the three members were still equal in power and made sure everyone knew that for all intents and purposes the alliance and the Aztec Empire were one and the same entity.

After Ahuitzotl died in 1502, his nephew, Montezuma II, became ruler of the vast Aztec realm, now at its zenith of power and influence. During Montezuma's first few years on the throne, the empire controlled possibly as many as five hundred separate Mesoamerican peoples and their respective nation-states. Collectively, this massive confederation supported somewhere between 5 million and 7 million people, close to three times the population of Britain and Wales at that same historical moment.

"The Spaniards possessed cannon and *arquebus* (primitive muskets) which terrified the American tribes."[11]

—Historian Edward Lawler

Tenochtitlán alone had some 200,000 residents, making it the most densely populated city ever to exist in Mesoamerica. Moreover, it was then one of the two or three biggest cities in the entire world. At that moment in time London had only 50,000 people; Spain's largest town, Granada, had 70,000; and Italy's leading city, Naples, had 114,000. Only Constantinople and Paris matched Tenochtitlán, with roughly 200,000 inhabitants each.

The Foundations of the Heavens

The master of Tenochtitlán and its empire, Montezuma II, proved to be a firm, even harsh ruler who often employed brutal tactics to keep his nobles and subjects in line. Had he been destined to deal only with fellow Mesoamerican enemies, he might have ended his reign as he had begun it—as a powerful and successful king. However, fate dealt Montezuma a very bad hand. He happened to be the Aztec ruler in

Conquests of the Aztec Kings

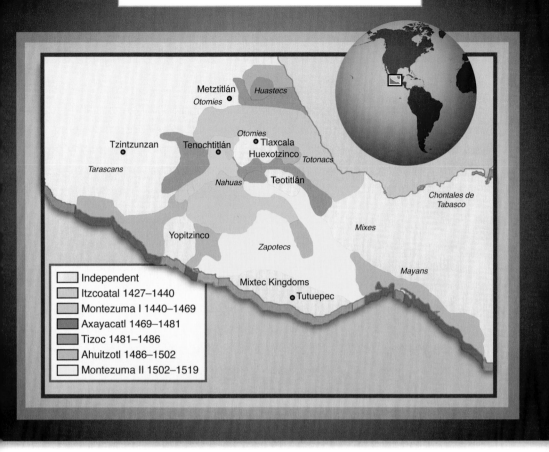

Metztitlán
Otomies
Huastecs
Otomies
Tzintzunzan
Tenochtitlán
Tlaxcala
Huexotzinco
Totonacs
Tarascans
Teotitlán
Nahuas
Chontales de
Tabasco
Mixes
Yopitzinco
Zapotecs
Mayans
Mixtec Kingdoms
Tutuepec

Independent
Itzcoatal 1427–1440
Montezuma I 1440–1469
Axayacatl 1469–1481
Tizoc 1481–1486
Ahuitzotl 1486–1502
Montezuma II 1502–1519

the year that Spanish military adventurer Hernán Cortés landed in eastern Mexico with an army of fewer than a thousand soldiers.

Despite the relatively small number of Spanish soldiers, in the space of only two years the Spaniards devastated the Aztecs and brought Mesoamerican civilization to its knees. A number of factors contributed to this lopsided victory, one of which was superior European military technology. According to USHistory.org historian Edward Lawler,

> The Spaniards possessed cannon and *arquebus* (primitive muskets) which terrified the American tribes. Horses, which the Aztecs had never encountered, gave the Spaniards greater mobility. Above all there was the Spanish sword. It could kill with a single lightning thrust. Against all this, the Aztec's primary weapons were wooden clubs studded with obsidian glass.[11]

The Aztec king Montezuma I was noted for expanding the realm controlled by the Triple Alliance into lands lying beyond the Valley of Mexico. Another of his major achievements was the creation of a set of written laws. After the Spanish conquest of Mexico, a Catholic friar, Diego Durán, preserved a copy of these laws, among them several that people today would view as overly strict. Excerpted here are numbers 1, 2, 4, 5, 7, 8, and 14 of Montezuma's statutes.

> 1. The king must never appear in public except when the occasion is extremely important and unavoidable. 2. Only the king may wear a golden diadem [crown] in the city. 4. Only the king is to wear the fine mantles [cloaks] of cotton embroidered with designs and threads of different colors and feather-work. 5. The great lords [nobles], who are twelve [in number], may wear special [cotton] mantles of certain make and design, and the minor lords, according to their valor and accomplishments, may wear others. 7. The commoners will not be allowed to wear cotton clothing, under pain of death, but can use only garments [made] of maguey fiber. 8. Only the great noblemen and valiant warriors are given license to build a house with a second story. For disobeying this law, a person receives the death penalty. 14. There is to be a rigorous law regarding adulterers. They are to be stoned and thrown into the rivers or to the buzzards.

Diego Durán, *The History of the Indies of New Spain*, trans. Doris Heyden. Norman: University of Oklahoma Press, 1994, pp. 209–10.

In addition, the Spaniards used the very nature of the Aztecs' supremacy over other native nations against them. Many Mesoamerican peoples who paid tribute to the kings ruling in Tenochtitlán resented the Aztecs and happily joined the foreigners in their march on that city. Historians estimate that up to 150,000 natives backed Cortés's small band of soldiers. Still another factor was that the Spaniards brought diseases, including smallpox and measles, with them. They had developed immunity to those plagues, but the Mesoamericans had not and died by the millions.

No one was more surprised by these dire events than the surviving Aztecs, who had always assumed that their capital was invincible and their nation destined to thrive forever. Not long before the Spaniards' arrival, an Aztec poet had composed a patriotic song that gave voice to those concepts. "Have this in mind," he warned potential rival cities and kings, and "do not forget it. Who could [ever] conquer Tenochtitlan? Who could shake the foundation of the heavens?"[12] Very soon after those lines were written, that once mighty city lay in ruins and the centuries-old Aztec civilization had reached an unexpectedly sudden and permanent end.

CHAPTER TWO

How Did Religion Spur the Aztec Migration into Mexico?

Focus Questions

1. How did religious beliefs influence the decisions and actions of Aztec kings? How might different beliefs have led to a different outcome?
2. What other mass migrations in human history have been guided by the belief, also held by the Aztecs, that departure from a homeland was ordained by a divinity? How might this belief have made the choice to leave easier?
3. What qualities and beliefs enabled the Aztecs to survive their long, perilous journey?

Evidence indicates that the Aztecs did not originate in central Mexico. Rather, it appears that they initially lived far to the north—possibly somewhere in the southwestern United States. Then, over time, probably during several generations, they migrated southward into the Valley of Mexico.

It was neither mere chance nor a sudden impulse that caused that fateful migration. Instead, the devout Aztecs listened to their priests, who, through traditional rituals, determined that a god wanted the migration to take place. That long journey and mass relocation of the Aztec people was destined to influence the courses of Mexican and European history in profound ways.

Reverence for the Divine

The role played by the Aztec priests in that epic scenario was clearly central. Indeed, based on what is known about the early Aztecs and their great migration, religion played a central role in both the migration and their lives in general. As was the case in many, if not most, ancient religions, the depth of people's faith was based on mutual give-and-take relationships with a god or gods.

The early Aztecs, for example, believed that certain divine beings provided good soil and periodic rains to water the crops grown in it. Those deities were also thought to ensure that the ocean and lakes teemed with fish and the forests were filled with game. In exchange for these gifts, which kept humans well fed, the Aztecs believed it was only right to repay those generous deities with regular worship. "The gods," researcher Guilhem Olivier explains, provided the Aztecs "with life, sustenance, and cultural benefits." In return, the Aztecs bestowed on their deities "prayers, songs, offerings and sacrifices."[13]

This unwavering dependence on and dedicated worship of heavenly beings was the centerpiece of Aztec religion. It produced a people so devout, Olivier points out, that after the Spanish conquest Christian friars were in nothing less than "utter awe" when they encountered the Aztecs. Those priests could not help but be impressed by the degree to which the natives expressed "a profound veneration of their gods."[14]

That strong reverence for the divine was shared by all members of Aztec society, whether rich and influential or poor and powerless. People worshipped both individually in private ceremonies and on a national scale in public ones. The leader of national worship was the king, known as the *tlatoani* in the Aztec language of Nahuatl. He expected his subjects to pray to and sacrifice in the name of various gods. In particular, by tradition he publicly praised and asked, on behalf of his people, for the support of Huitzilopochtli, the Aztecs' patron deity and the stern and at times bloodthirsty god of war and human sacrifice.

In addition to prayer and sacrifice (of animals and plants as well as humans), the Aztecs honored their gods by taking part in annual religious festivals. In that way and in others, their sacred rituals

> "[The Aztec gods] are better viewed as invisible spirits or forces whose roles, natures, and forms blended together."[15]
>
> —Historian Michael E. Smith

resembled those of a number of ancient and medieval European peoples. One major difference was the manner in which the Aztecs (and other Mesoamerican peoples) envisioned the deities they worshipped. The Greeks and Romans, for example, pictured their gods in human form. In contrast, Smith explains, the Aztec gods "are better viewed as invisible spirits or forces whose roles, natures, and forms blended together."[15]

This copy of an illustration from an Aztec codex captures one of the bloody human sacrifices to the war deity Huitzilopochtli. After tearing out a victim's heart, a priest tossed the corpse down the temple's steps.

The God's Order and Pledge

Aztecs of all walks of life harbored a seemingly limitless devotion to their invisible but all-powerful gods. As a result, when the priests announced that they had detected natural signs of the divine will, everyone took it seriously and was ready to bow to that will. According to the Aztecs' cherished myth describing their great migration, this is what occurred in the dim past when they dwelled in Aztlan. The local priests claimed that Huitzilopochtli had ordered the entire population to leave the tribal homeland and journey far to the south.

This story presents historians with two challenges. First, it is part of an ancient myth, and many myths have little or no factual basis. A natural question, therefore, is how much credibility should scholars give to the tale? As it turns out, many modern experts agree that a fair number of incidents described in the myth are based on real events. Archaeological, linguistic, and other evidence shows that the Aztecs did migrate into the Valley of Mexico from somewhere far to the north. So the chances of Aztlan being a garbled memory of a real place are high.

That brings scholars to their second challenge; namely, where was Aztlan? Those experts who have studied the ancient evidence have proposed several possible geographical locations. Some are in north-central Mexico, but others lie farther north, in what is now the American Southwest. Some scholars see a close link between Nahuatl and the language of the Utes, a Native American tribe inhabiting Utah and Colorado. Still other investigators favor part of Arizona as the original site of Aztlan.

That legendary land's real location aside, experts agree that religious devotion compelled the Aztecs to follow the order they earnestly believed Huitzilopochtli had given them—to migrate southward. The deity pledged that he would keep a close eye on them during the expedition. Also, he said, there was no need for haste. They could erect temporary towns now and then during the journey, in which they would construct makeshift homes of whatever natural materials they could find. For a while, they would naturally sustain themselves by clearing some fields and growing whatever crops they required. Then, after a few years the people would abandon the impermanent town and continue southward.

After all, the god continued, the Aztecs' ultimate fate was to create a permanent and magnificent new city and nation in a spot the great Huitzilopochtli had chosen. When they had reached their final destination, he said, he would provide an unmistakable sign. They should be on the lookout for a handsome eagle perched on a cactus growing out of a rock. There, the god assured them, they would finally find their well-deserved rest and establish a grand new life. In that place, their name would thereafter be honored throughout the known world, and the Aztec nation would become truly great. "The might of our arms," Huitzilopochtli declared, "will be known along with the courage of our brave hearts. With these we shall conquer nations, near and distant, we shall subdue towns and cities from sea to sea. We shall become lords of gold and silver, of jewels and precious stones, [and we will] call this place Tenochtitlan. There we will build the city that is to be queen, that is to rule over all others in the country."[16]

Erecting Temporary Settlements

Tradition held that the Aztecs departed Aztlan on the Great Journey ordained by their war god in the year 1122 CE. To show their undying devotion to Huitzilopochtli and remind the common folk that he was always present, the priests carried along a statue of him. They stored it in a container made of river reeds and put it on public display from time to time. When this happened, the people gathered around the statue, bowed low, and offered the deity prayers of thanks for guiding them toward their ultimate and rightful destiny.

During the long journey, the Aztecs followed Huitzilopochtli's initial directives and stopped now and then to erect temporary settlements. The homes they constructed were made of the same materials they would later employ in the building of large portions of Tenochtitlán. The design and layout of a house depended on the wealth and social standing of the family that dwelled in it. The homes were of two main types—the ones in which the relatively few nobles resided, and those of average people, who made up the bulk of the population.

> "We shall conquer nations, near and distant, we shall subdue towns and cities from sea to sea."[16]
>
> —Attributed to the Aztec god Huitzilopochtli

Aztec aristocrats and other wealthy individuals most often lived in roomy two-story dwellings constructed over sturdy stone foundations. The walls consisted of bricks made of clay hardened by fire and/or fieldstones of various sizes. The builders then covered these sturdy materials with a layer of plaster, which could be left unpainted or painted in bright colors. Such a home typically featured several rooms, among them a combination foyer and meeting room, a dining chamber, and multiple bedrooms. Most rooms opened into a central courtyard. Open to the elements, it usually had a bathing pool, sitting areas, and flower gardens.

In stark contrast, Aztec commoners most often inhabited very small houses that rarely featured more than two rooms. They were

The Aztecs were talented builders. Some of their typical construction methods are displayed here, including thatch (top left) used in average people's houses, and various types of arches employed in stone buildings.

made from clay bricks, but not the fairly expensive fired kind used for the walls of richer homes. Poorer folk had to rely on the cheaper process of packing the clay into wooden molds and leaving them out in the sun to dry.

In some commoners' homes the largest room was dominated by a brick-lined hearth that doubled as a cooking area and heating source to warm the occupants on cold nights. Other lower-class families placed their hearth in a small separate shed located a few feet from the main hut. Family members slept on mats composed of woven reeds and employed similar mats as rugs to cover the otherwise dirt floors.

The fact that most Aztec houses were relatively small and made of easily gathered natural materials worked to the advantage of

A Deep Connection with the Natural World

One of the more distinctive features of Aztec religion was the strong and deep connection between humans and the natural world that they believed was tightly controlled by the gods. To the average Aztec, those deities oversaw the many interconnected aspects of the natural landscape. According to Harvard University scholar David Carrasco, "All of life was considered inherently sacred and literally filled with the potency of divine beings. The gods were expressions of the sacred powers that permeated the world." Moreover, for an Aztec, the word for a god—*teotl*—"signified a sacred power manifested in natural forms, such as a tree, a mountain, or a rainstorm, [or] in mysterious and chaotic places, such as caves, whirlpools, or storms."

Based on these beliefs, the Aztecs made honoring the natural world's sacred features an integral part of their daily lives. Perhaps the most obvious example of this religious dedication was how the Aztecs chose the location for their capital, Tenochtitlán. They built it in the midst of Lake Texcoco not simply because they enjoyed being surrounded by beautiful scenery. Rather, the choice was made on the basis of the fact that the lake was considered one of the most sacred natural places in the known world.

David Carrasco, *Daily Life of the Aztecs*. Santa Barbara, CA: ABC-CLIO, 2011, p. 48.

the migrating tribe. Such structures took little time to build, so a moderate-sized temporary town could be erected in a few weeks. While some people constructed houses, others fashioned corrals for the sheep and goats they had brought with them and cleared nearby fields so they would produce one or more seasons of crops.

The First Human Sacrifices?

Eventually, the traveling tribe reached a place in Mexico called Coatepec, the exact location of which is still unknown. According to the myth of the great migration, the Aztecs stayed in the area for at least thirty years. There, they not only built a temporary town but also diverted the waters of a local river, thereby making a small lake. In addition, they constructed a temple dedicated to Huitzilopochtli atop a hill, which became sacred in Aztec lore. (Later, in Tenochtitlán, the Great Temple, also honoring Huitzilopochtli, was meant to be a replica of the holy mound at Coatepec.)

The stop at Coatepec turned out to be different than earlier ones in another way. Namely, some members of the group eventually decided it was time to move on, but this time others, including several priests, rebelled. They said they wanted to end their incessant travels and live permanently beside the artificial lake they had created. In the migration myth, Huitzilopochtli became enraged and punished the rebels by ripping out their hearts.

A number of modern scholars have suggested that this bloody episode in the story is likely a muddled recollection of a real event in which two competing groups of Aztecs fought for dominance. The winners seem to have decided that their opponents had betrayed Huitzilopochtli and therefore deserved to be slaughtered. Because the victims had offended the god, it was necessary that their deaths be part of formal religious rituals connected to that deity. Many historians believe that this mass sacrifice, involving the removal of hearts, may have marked the start of the Aztecs' infamous custom of human sacrifice.

After the execution of the rebels, the surviving Aztecs departed Coatepec and resumed their southward trek. As near as modern experts can tell, during the late 1200s the intrepid band reached the northern edge of expansive Lake Texcoco. It was immediately clear that the region was already peopled by a number of native groups. Moreover, almost all of those small nation-states were militarily superior to the Aztecs and viewed them with suspicion. Several groups warned the newcomers to keep their distance; in response, the Aztecs kept on moving and steadily made their way around the enormous waterway's western shore.

The Journey's End

After the passage of an unknown number of weeks or months, the wandering Aztecs suddenly came upon a place called Chapultepec, meaning "Grasshopper Hill." There they constructed a village with a wooden

An early modern Mexican painting depicts one of the most important moments in Aztec mythology—when the wandering Aztecs found an eagle perched on a cactus. Supposedly this was a divine sign that they had found their permanent home.

stockade surrounding it in order to protect themselves from periodic attacks by nearby hostile natives. Even that barrier did not stop the assaults, however. So the suffering pilgrims felt compelled to move again.

The Aztecs now traversed the lake's southern shore. Shortly afterward, in about 1299, they arrived on the eastern shore and entered the small city-state of Colhuacan. The local king, Cocoxtli, was the first ruler in the region to take pity on the new arrivals. He permitted the Aztecs to inhabit a rocky, largely barren patch of his territory, and they did their best to make it livable. Just as they had done numerous times in the years after leaving Aztlan, they built houses to shelter themselves and managed to grow the food they required.

This period in which the Aztecs occupied another people's land did not last long. Only a few years after Cocoxtli had allowed them to camp on his land, he and they had a falling out; again, the Aztecs were forced to leave their homes and go on the move.

The Aztecs' relentless, perilous journey continued until 1325. At some point that year, the migration story claims, they wandered slowly through some forested land very near Lake Texcoco. After exiting a dense grove of trees and undergrowth, they suddenly found themselves on the lakeshore and saw that the water there was unusually clear. What is more, the flowers in the area were both abundant and beautiful.

The Origins of the Great Journey Story

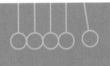

The story of the Aztec migration from Aztlan reached the modern world through a torturous process. The Aztecs were a literate people and their scribes produced a large number of written documents, including ones relating to the gods and various myths. Included were writings recounting the story of the so-called Great Journey, in which the early Aztecs migrated into the Valley of Mexico. Unfortunately for later generations, the vast majority of original Aztec writings were destroyed during or shortly after the Spanish conquest of the early 1520s. In fact, an undetermined but reportedly large proportion of those native documents were destroyed in 1535 in a bonfire ordered by Spanish priest Juan de Zumárraga. On a more positive note, a few of the Spanish priests, who were also scholars, regretted the loss of most Aztec literature. These priests interviewed surviving Aztecs and wrote down accounts in Spanish of various myths and other stories and facts relating to Aztec culture. Among the Spanish scribes were Bernardino de Sahagún and Diego Durán. Thanks to these men, more than twenty versions of the Great Journey were committed to writing. In addition, another account of the myth was created by King Montezuma II's grandson, Fernando de Alvarado Tezozómoc. Each version of the tale differed in a few details from the others. But they all agreed that the Aztecs originally came from a place called Aztlan, situated far to the north of the Valley of Mexico.

A few minutes later, the people in the tribe's front ranks came upon a scene that filled them with a mixture of awe, relief, and joy. It was a large rock with a prickly pear cactus growing out of its summit. Above the cactus stood a magnificent eagle, the story goes, "with its wings stretched out toward the rays of the sun, basking in their warmth and the freshness of the morning. In his talons he held a bird with very fine feathers, precious and shining." (The bird the eagle was eating was changed to a snake after the Spaniards conquered Mexico.) Seeing this, the Aztecs "humbled themselves" and bowed down "as if the bird were a divine thing." Then, on catching sight of them, the great winged creature

> "As the Aztecs observed the actions of the eagle, they realized they had come to the end of their journey."[17]
>
> —Spanish friar Diego Durán

also humbled himself, bowing his head low in their direction. As the Aztecs observed the actions of the eagle, they realized they had come to the end of their journey, so they began to weep and dance about with joy and contentment. In thanksgiving, they said, "By what right do we deserve such good fortune? Who made us worthy of such grace, such excellence, and greatness?"[17]

Happier than they had been in living memory, the Aztecs felt certain they knew the answer to that question. Their divine patron, Huitzilopochtli, had led them to the glorious fate he had decreed for them. They had remained faithful to him and he had returned the favor. This part of the migration story, some historians have pointed out, corresponds to one of the often recorded aspects of Aztec society and life. As a people they felt special, even exceptional. That feeling was based on the firm belief that one of the strongest of the gods had chosen them above other peoples. This belief later supported their claims that they were superior and destined to rule the known world.

CHAPTER THREE

How Did Reverence for the Gods Shape the Aztecs' Creative Expression?

Focus Questions

1. Why might people be interested in creating masks, as the Aztecs did?
2. Why do you think human societies build ornate places of worship such as those constructed by the Aztecs?
3. In your view, why do most societies use religious concepts like the Aztecs did to explain what might exist after death?

The Aztecs produced a rich array of decorative arts, including painting, sculpture, and architecture, along with literature. These artistic disciplines were not simply the expressions of a creative people. They were also laced with religious symbolism, revealing that religious faith drove, or at least strongly guided, much of the Aztecs' creativity. In fact, most Aztec art was specifically designed to appeal more to the gods than to humans. As Eduardo M. Moctezuma points out, "For the Westerner, all the [artistic] work is to be seen. It is a dialogue between humans. For the Aztec in ancient Mexico, it had another character—it was a dialogue with the gods."[18]

Views of Aztec Art Through the Eyes of Their Conquerors

This dialogue with divine powers, along with most Aztec art in general, was not closely studied and appreciated until well into the modern era. In large part this is because the Spaniards portrayed the native Mesoamericans the way conquerors often portray conquered peoples—in an unfavorable light. But more than that, the Europeans of the period considered the Aztecs and their neighbors to be socially and culturally inferior to themselves.

As researcher Julia Flood explains, in the decades following the Spanish conquest of Mexico, Spanish writings about the Aztecs made uniformly negative judgments about that native people's character. Those "writings express how misguided and barbaric" the Spaniards "thought their Mexican charges to be in their worship of multiple gods." Most Spanish priests "thought many Aztec practices to be base and even evil." Moreover, many Spaniards considered the conquered natives "to be more akin to animals than thoughtful, conscious beings."[19] Because Aztec art was integral to supposedly corrupt and barbaric Aztec culture, for many years most Europeans assumed it was equally unworthy and disregarded it.

> "[To many Spaniards, the Aztecs were] more akin to animals than thoughtful, conscious beings."[19]
>
> —Researcher Julia Flood

Views like these made it practically impossible for the conquering Spaniards to recognize the complexity and richness of Aztec culture. They failed to see the sophisticated architecture, sculpture, painting, ceramics, and literature that were part of that culture. Similarly, they had no idea that the Mesoamerican peoples had studied astronomy and mathematics and had created calendars based on those sciences.

Another reason why early modern Spaniards and other Europeans tended to ignore or disparage Aztec art and literature was that those creations were conceptually unlike their European counterparts. Sixteenth-century European art certainly had strong religious dimensions. But paintings or sculptures of religious subjects were designed to appeal to and move human viewers. In contrast, Aztec art—also heavy in religious themes and symbolism—was intended to appeal more to divine eyes and sensibilities.

An example of this approach to art can be seen in large numbers of Aztec wall paintings and architectural decorations. In these works, researcher Jaime Cóttrill states, "the gods were often depicted, and they themselves often resembled animals of various kinds. The drawings of the gods were often sharp and angular, brightly colored. Art

Fascinated with astronomy, the Aztecs used the sun's and planets' movements to mark the passage of time by creating calendar stones like this now famous one discovered in the remains of Tenochtitlán in 1789.

would often show gods, or priests dressed as gods in a ritual."[20] Art experts point out that the renderings in question contain a distinctive combination of exaggerated and even abstract features. This was a sort of visual language meant to be understood not by humans but by gods. Another example of this approach can be seen in Aztec statues. Their bottoms, which human observers would never see, were carved in minute detail because of the belief that heavenly deities *could* see those parts of the statues.

Large-Scale Religious Structures

Much like the Aztecs' paintings and statues, their principal architecture was intended to honor and impress the gods. Here, it is important to differentiate Aztec and other Mesoamerican architecture, along with ancient European architecture, from modern versions. Today, all sorts of structures—from skyscrapers and other office buildings to department stores and individual houses—are individually designed and seen as examples of formal architecture.

In ancient Mexico, Egypt, Mesopotamia, and Greece, in comparison, most people's homes were very small and thrown together with perishable materials such as tree branches, thatch (bundled plant stems), and dried mud bricks. They were at the time, and still are today, not viewed as formal architectural forms. In Mesoamerica and other ancient lands, formal architecture was almost always confined to monumental structures composed of stone and/or other more durable materials.

The most important and visually impressive of those edifices in ancient cities, including those in Aztec-dominated Mesoamerica, were temples dedicated to the gods. In the Aztec capital of Tenochtitlán and many other Mesoamerican cities, the temples were called *teocalli*, literally meaning "god houses." They were by far the largest, most splendid, and most long-lasting buildings. They were typically erected in spacious plazas that historians often call ceremonial centers. Here, the term *ceremonial* denotes activities connected to religious ideas, beliefs, and rituals. (It must be pointed out, however, that such centers had secondary purposes, notably to serve as propaganda—that is, to impress rival peoples with the Aztec realm's military and cultural might.)

The main architectural form relating to temples in the Aztec ceremonial centers was a large four-sided pyramid that was truncated, or leveled off, at the top. (In contrast, Egyptian pyramids came to a point at the summit.) Aztec pyramids were not in and of themselves temples, but rather one or more temples were placed on a pyramid's truncated top. Another distinctive feature of such a structure was a steep staircase built into one of its sides. Stone railings called balustrades ran along the sides of the staircase.

Some Aztec temple-pyramids had two staircases. The best-known example was the Great Temple, or Templo Mayor, that dominated Tenochtitlán's central area and skyline. Cóttrill describes its look and basic functions, saying that

> it had two shrines on the top—one to Huitzilopochtli and one to Tlaloc. Huitzilopochtli was the patron god of the Mexica [Aztec] people, the one who led them to Tenochtitlan in the first place. He was the god of the sun and war. Tlaloc was

the god of rain and fertility. [Many] rituals were done at the temple—human sacrifice, of course, is the most well known. But there were many more, such as private ritual blood-letting, burning of copal (a tree resin), and the music of worship.[21]

Another frequent aspect of Aztec religiously oriented architecture was the practice of overbuilding. On a number of occasions the ruling elite decided to construct a new pyramid on the same site as an

The ceramic urn pictured here was found within the rubble of the great temple in Tenochtitlán dedicated partly to the rain god Tlaloc. The fierce, hideous, demon-like face is that of Tlaloc himself, at least as the Aztecs envisioned him.

existing one. In such a situation today, the builders would first hire a demolition crew to tear down the older structure. The Aztec approach was very different. In Tenochtitlán and other Aztec cities, the builders added new materials "over the existing edifice," scholar Manuel Aguilar-Moreno explains:

> The result would be a new temple that was larger, more extravagant, and more detailed. Enlarging preexisting structures meant adding more stairs and making the sacrificial area more spacious. Layering a preexisting temple was acceptable because the gods had already blessed the original temple. In fact, building a more magnificent temple paid further tribute to the gods.[22]

Aztec Ceramics

Although far smaller than temple-pyramids, Aztec ceramics were no less well designed. Ceramic items were produced in large numbers each year by talented Aztec craftspeople—and were often equal in quality to European clay pottery made during the same centuries.

Aztec ceramics were, on the one hand, practical. Typical were cups, vases, bowls, dishes, incense burners, and funerary urns used by people every day. On the other hand, there were also religious dimensions to Aztec ceramics. First, a great many of the useful ceramics made in Aztec communities featured painted decorations. The earliest versions were fairly simple motifs and patterns, such as dark borders, dots, and swirls. But beginning shortly after the founding of Tenochtitlán in the 1320s, potters started painting naturalistic images of flowers and plants, butterflies, birds, rabbits, fish, and other living things. In many cases, these images were symbols representing specific deities.

"The result would be a new temple that was larger, more extravagant, and more detailed."[22]

—Scholar Manuel Aguilar-Moreno on Aztec building techniques

For instance, a flower, or *xochitl*, stood for the god of storytelling and dance, Huehuecoyotl. Similarly, a rabbit, or *tochtli*, represented the fertility goddess Mayahuel, and a snake, or *coatl*, stood for Chalchiuhtlicue, the goddess of oceans and rivers.

The exact reasons why symbols of gods appeared on ceramics are somewhat uncertain. But many experts think that the Aztecs' high degree of religious devotion played a part. It is possible that rulers and other members of the upper classes expected potters to add such symbols to remind people that the gods were everywhere and always watching them.

Another religious dimension to pottery making was that a fair number of ceramic items were created specifically to be used in religious rituals. These included large ceremonial bowls into which priests drained blood or placed hearts ripped from victims of human sacrifice. There were also ceramic architectural decorations that graced the temples where sacrifices took place. Perhaps the most striking of those adornments were life-size figures of gods and human warriors who fought on behalf of the deities. Moctezuma describes two such soldier statues that stood in a temple in Tenochtitlán and remarks that because they were so large it was customary to fashion them in four interlocking sections:

> The head, the chest and arms, the abdomen and the thighs, and finally the legs were fitted together to make up these impressive ceramic warriors. The face of the individual inside the bird's head, with its enormous beak, is a brilliant example of Aztec aesthetics [artistic feelings and expression]. The total expression of these figures is not only an example of the extent of utilization of clay the Aztecs achieved, but it [also] succeeds in reproducing the dignity and fierce quality of the warriors of [the war god] Huitzilopochtli.[23]

Masks and Other Crafts

Of the other Aztec crafts, mask making was one of the more colorful. For a reminder that many other premodern peoples made masks, one need turn only to the ancient Greeks, whose actors wore them on stage. The Aztecs, in contrast, had no formal theater. But they employed masks in several other social areas, most notably in religious rituals. As Cóttrill explains, these finely crafted artworks "were used for worship of the gods, whether by being displayed in a temple or

The World's Largest Pyramid

When most people hear the words *ancient pyramid*, they think first of Egypt's famous Great Pyramid of Giza, the enormous stone tomb of the early pharaoh Khufu. A common assumption is that the Great Pyramid is the biggest pyramid ever constructed, but this notion is actually incorrect. The largest ancient pyramid is one located in the ancient Mexican town of Cholula. The Cholula pyramid was used for religious rituals by generations of Aztecs. Situated near the modern city of Puebla (in south-central Mexico), the Cholula pyramid has a base four times larger than that of Khufu's tomb. According to researcher Josh Hrala of the scientific news website ScienceAlert, the Cholula structure is often overlooked because it is

> hidden beneath layers of dirt, making it look more like a natural mountain than a place of worship. [In order] to understand how awesome the Great Pyramid of Cholula is, we must jump back to [when] it was built in around 300 BCE by many different communities to honor the ancient god Quetzalcoatl. [The] pyramid was likely constructed with adobe, a type of brick made out of baked mud, and it features six layers built on top of each other over many generations. [This] incremental growth is what allowed the Great Pyramid of Cholula to get so big. [At] roughly 66 meters (217 feet) tall, the pyramid's total volume is about 4.45 million cubic meters (157 million cubic feet), while the Great Pyramid of Giza's volume is just 2.5 million cubic meters (88.2 million cubic feet).

Josh Hrala, "The World's Largest Pyramid Is Hidden Under a Mountain in Mexico," ScienceAlert. www.sciencealert.com.

worn by a priest." He goes on to note that "they usually represented one god or another, and the Aztecs did have many gods." For example, "a common type of mask would have snakes on it, a representation of the god Quetzalcoatl or perhaps Tlaloc."[24]

The Aztecs also applied their artistry to death masks. Surprisingly, they did not usually place such masks directly over the faces of deceased individuals, as was common in ancient European societies. Instead, Aztec death masks, typically featuring closed eyes and an open mouth, were most commonly worn by nobles during or after ceremonies honoring the memory of a person who had died.

The Aztecs fashioned their masks from a wide variety of materials. Turquoise, a fairly rare and therefore valuable mineral, was frequently used in mask making because it was seen as a sacred stone. This seemed a logical choice considering that masks were so often employed for religious purposes. Wood, green-colored stones, and the dark volcanic stone obsidian were also regularly used to create masks. Common as well was covering those base materials with colorful mosaics composed of small pieces of shell, coral, turquoise, jade, obsidian, and/or gold.

Other crafts at which the Aztecs excelled included wood carving, jewelry making, and feather work. In fact, the artistic application of bird feathers, originally copied from the Toltecs, was one of the most widespread and respected crafts in Aztec-controlled Mesoamerica. Artisans chose vibrantly colored feathers from several of the many bird species native to Mexico, among them the squirrel cuckoo, heron, egret, roseate spoonbill, macaw, quetzal, and golden eagle.

It was believed that these feathers had magical properties connected to the divine powers wielded by the gods. So a religious ceremonial quality was often attached to their use. Therefore, feathers decorated the headdresses of priests and kings, the arrows and shields of warriors, and the formal outfits worn by nobles. In addition, soldiers killed in battle were often buried with feathers. It was hoped that their magical properties would induce the gods to look favorably on the souls of the deceased men. Also due to their perceived powerful properties, rare feathers were routinely used in political diplomacy. Shortly after the Spaniards landed in Mexico in 1519, for example, the Aztec king sent their leader, Cortés, the gift of a headdress featuring more than five hundred feathers.

A Medium for Recording and Learning

Writing was another important art form frequently used by the Aztecs to appeal to, appease, or honor the gods. All Aztec priests and nobles, along with at least a few commoners, could read and write, which was a high rate of literacy for a premodern people. For the

Aztecs, literature was a medium through which they recorded and learned about their history and myths, which were often one and the same. They also recorded many of their poems and religious hymns in writing.

Most Aztec books were of a type that scholars call a codex. A typical codex consisted of several long strips of paper, which was made from dried deer hide and the inner bark of fig trees. One placed the

One kind of calendar the Aztecs employed is shown in this illustration from the codex now called the Borbonicus. Arrayed along the outer edges of the square are the days of the month and the deities associated with them.

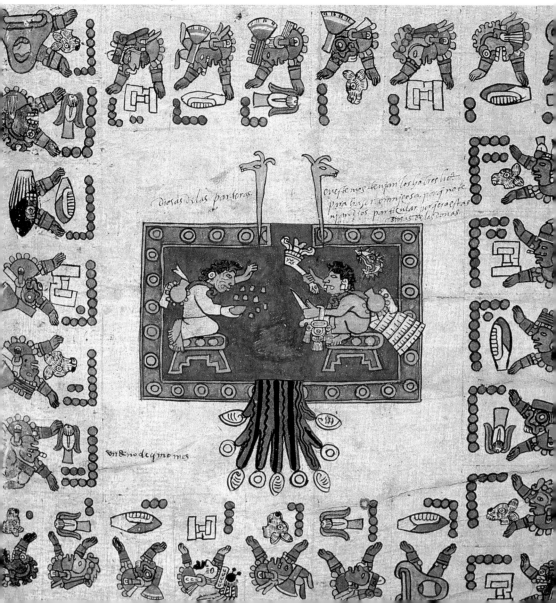

"Would That One Lived Forever"

One of the central religious questions asked by the Aztecs (as well as by virtually all human societies) was what happens to people after death? That the Aztecs addressed this weighty topic is proven by the existence of a surviving poem dating from the era of the Triple Alliance. The work expresses sadness that human life is so short and wonders at how mystifying and uncertain life after death seems to be.

> One day we must go [that is, die].
> One night we will descend into the region of mystery.
> Here, we only come to know ourselves.
> Only in passing are we here on Earth.
> In peace and pleasure let us spend our lives.
> Come, let us enjoy ourselves.
> Let not the angry do so. The Earth is vast indeed!
> Would that one lived forever. Would that one were not to die!

Quoted in Miguel León-Portilla, *Aztec Thought and Culture*. Norman: University of Oklahoma Press, 1990, p. 73.

bark in boiling water until it was very soft, dried it, and then pounded it with a stone hammer into thin sheets. To fashion a codex, one folded these sheets in a zigzag or accordion-like manner so that they would unfold when the book opened.

The books consisted of a combination of pictograms and glyphs. Pictograms are pictures that literally represent various objects, as when an image of part of a coiled snake stands for a snake. Glyphs, or logograms, are abstract or picture-like signs that stand for words, names, or concepts. The meaning of some Aztec concept glyphs are obvious; for example, an image of a corpse wrapped in a burial shroud represents death, and a club and shield signify war. The meaning of other concept glyphs is a bit more cryptic. A cluster of three footprints does not signify the obvious "feet," for instance, but rather means "walking." Similarly, the image of a burning temple means "conquest." In this system, a place name often consists of a cluster of two or three pictograms. A good example is the Aztec capital of Tenochtitlán, represented by little pictures of a stone and a cactus (a reference to the cactus growing from the stone in the city's foundation myth).

> "No one is like unto him. Not vainly do I sing his praises."[25]
>
> —From an Aztec hymn to the war god Huitzilopochtli

At first glance, the use of images in Aztec writing might seem too simple or general to express complex thoughts. In practice, however, that way of writing was more than sufficient for the needs of a premodern agricultural society. Their writing was certainly sophisticated enough to allow the Aztecs to create their most cherished written expressions—hymns to their gods. The following example is part of a surviving ode to the war deity Huitzilopochtli:

Huitzilopochtli is first in rank. No one, no one is like unto him. Not vainly do I sing his praises, [for] he is a terror to the Mixteca [a people the Aztecs conquered]; he alone destroyed the Picha-Huasteca. He conquered them. The Dart-Hurler [one of the god's nicknames] is an example to the city, as he sets to work. [When] he shouts aloud he inspires great terror, the divine hurler, the god turning himself in the combat![25]

Along with erecting towering temples, fashioning statues of the gods, and offering those deities finely crafted masks and feather work, composing such hymns clearly demonstrated the strong religious undertones of nearly all Aztec artistic creations.

CHAPTER FOUR

How Did Warfare Define the Aztecs' Identity and Success as a People?

Focus Questions

1. What reasons might societies have for honoring their military heroes as the Aztecs did?
2. What might be the advantage of forcing one's neighbors to pay tribute rather than conquering and ruling them?
3. What are the advantages and disadvantages of allowing rulers to personally participate in battles as the Aztec kings did?

Like the Assyrians in ancient Mesopotamia and the Spartans in ancient Greece, the Aztecs of Mesoamerica placed war and military culture in a far more prominent place in their culture than most historical peoples did. Warrior-oriented institutions and values were highly integrated into all political and social aspects of Aztec society. Indeed, Manuel Aguilar-Moreno points out that "an Aztec male's identity was defined by his success in warfare." Moreover, "even in female identity, warfare was important. Childbirth was compared to combat." Military culture was also well integrated into the education of young men and could help determine a person's social status, Aguilar-Moreno explains:

Male education [strongly] emphasized military skills and values, and the main aim of [many schools] was to create warriors. Although social status in Aztec society was largely predetermined by family lineage, warfare provided a means of climbing the social ladder. Young warriors elevated their social status by taking captives in battle, and more important, they secured that status for their descendants.[26]

The Reasons for Fighting Wars

In fact, a warrior who made several such captures, plus otherwise distinguished himself in battle, could attain a degree of social rank almost as high as his military general or a high priest. (Both of those lofty offices ranked directly below that of the king himself in the social pecking order). Furthermore, a warrior who had attained such high honors could expect to receive a number of different kinds of positive compensation.

For example, not long after the Spaniards conquered the Aztecs, a Spanish priest wrote that illustrious Aztec warriors were widely praised by people of all walks of life. They also received all sorts of favors and valuable gifts. Such a successful warrior was summoned to the royal court, the priest recalled, where the king "gave him his honor." The hair on the warrior's head "was parted in two, and a red cord wrapped around it. In the same cord was attached an ornament of green, blue, and red feathers."[27] This tribute was special indeed considering that a feathered headdress was viewed as a gift befitting a king or a god.

> "Young [Aztec] warriors elevated their social status by taking captives in battle."[26]
>
> —Historian Manuel Aguilar-Moreno

When these decorated combatants and the other Aztec soldiers fought in battle, most often they were not trying to gain new lands for their nation to own and rule, as was customary in Europe. Instead, their principal goal was to turn an enemy nation into a subject state that would thereafter be required to pay annual tribute to the Aztec government. That ensured that the Aztecs would receive a stable, ongoing supply of valuable items, including weapons, semiprecious stones, food, building materials, fabrics, ceramic objects, paper, and more.

To acquire a new subject state that would provide such useful forms of tribute, the Aztec monarch and his advisers followed a set

These drawings show Aztec soldiers. The one at lower right is protected by body armor. The others carry various kinds of weapons, including war clubs and swords, and all wear ornamented headdresses and carry small circular shields.

political ritual. In both theory and practice its aim was, if possible, to avoid actual warfare in which many would die on both sides. First, the king sent envoys to the enemy king and urged him to surrender peacefully. If that leader refused to submit, another Aztec ambassador

Soldiers with the "Look of Devils"

Spanish historian Francisco López de Gómara lived in the same era in which his countryman Hernán Cortés invaded Mexico. López de Gómara wrote a treatise based in part on eyewitness accounts by some of Cortés's troops. Among other things, the work describes one of several Mesoamerican armies that Cortés's men saw in action during the nearly three years following the initial Spanish landing in September 1519. "The men were splendidly armed in their fashion and their faces were painted" with red body paint, López de Gómara wrote. The red hue in a sense

> gave them the look of devils. They carried plumes and maneuvered marvelously well. Their weapons were slings, pikes, lances, swords, and bows and arrows. [They also had] helmets [and] arm and leg armor of wood gilded or covered with feathers or leather. Their breastplates were of cotton. Their shields [which were] very handsome and not at all weak, were of tough wood and leather, with brass and feather ornaments. Their swords [were] of wood with [pieces of sharpened] flint set into them, which cut well and made a nasty wound. Their troops were arranged in squadrons, each with many trumpets, conches [seashells], and drums, all of which was a sight to see.

Quoted in Hammond Innes, *The Conquistadors*. New York: Knopf, 1972, p. 81.

paid him a visit and warned that if he would not surrender, he and his people would pay an awful price. The fearsome Aztec army would visit death and destruction on his land and its occupants.

Many Mesoamerican peoples heeded such warnings and agreed to pay the Aztecs tribute. Only if a targeted nation-state firmly declined to surrender without a fight did the Aztec king take the final step. When he determined he must go to war, his military generals sent messengers throughout Tenochtitlán and into the smaller towns and villages surrounding it. These heralds called on Aztec males who were seventeen or older to leave their families and jobs behind for the time being. They were expected to serve in the military for a few weeks or perhaps longer. They knew that when the upcoming campaign was over they could return to their homes and occupations. (This made them a militia—a force of temporary fighters—rather than professional soldiers.)

Aztec women were not usually expected or asked to fight in battle. If and when the homeland came under direct attack, however, they did fight alongside their brothers and husbands. Moreover, there were Aztec tales of women who served in the army with uncommon skill and bravery.

In addition, Aztec leaders sometimes used women in strategic ways. A famous example occurred when the Spaniards laid siege to Tenochtitlán during the early 1520s. When he deemed it necessary, King Montezuma II told thousands of women to go to the rooftops of their houses and with loud voices warn away the intruders. This approach was at least momentarily effective. The Spanish priest Diego Durán later recalled, "When Cortes saw the great number of people covering the flat roofs and filling the streets of the city, he became afraid and feared that he would not be able to conquer Mexico."[28]

Weapons Wielded with Amazing Force

When word came to Aztec men that a military campaign was about to begin, they immediately gathered their weapons and armor. As children, males received extensive training from their fathers in a wide array of offensive weapons. So they achieved a high level of skill with the standard tools of war by the time they were seventeen and eligible to serve.

Among those weapons, one of the more effective and lethal was the atlatl. Basically a throwing stick, it measured about 18 inches (46 cm) long and consisted mainly of a wooden handle bearing a thin furrow, or groove. The soldier wielding it slipped a dart or short spear into the furrow and then fired the weapon by flipping the stick in a vigorous overhand motion. The atlatl was effective because it provided an ordinary spear with considerably more power than a person could manage to produce with his or her arm alone. Another advantage was that a soldier could use it with one hand. That permitted him to fend off an opponent with one arm while helping a wounded companion with the other.

Still another reason why the atlatl was so deadly was that the average Mesoamerican male (and some women as well) became highly skilled at using it at a fairly young age. In fact, the Aztecs were more expert in the use of the atlatl than most Europeans were with swords. For this reason, numerous Spaniards were awed when they witnessed native Mexicans using the atlatl. One Spanish soldier, Garcilaso de la Vega, saw the weapon's use in actual battle. He later reported that it was "capable of sending a dart with such great force that it has been seen to pass completely through a man armed with a coat of [armor]."[29]

> "It has been seen to pass completely through a man armed with a coat of [armor]."[29]
>
> —Spanish soldier Garcilaso de la Vega on the dart from an atlatl

The Aztecs used other projectile, or missile, weapons as well. Among them were bows and arrows, spears, and diverse kinds of slings. A Mesoamerican sling fired smooth stones up to the incredible distance of 660 feet (201 m). Moreover, a stone hurled from such a sling traveled extremely quickly—faster than the fastest fastball of a baseball pitcher—and did substantial damage to the human body. A highly impressed Spaniard who witnessed Mesoamerican slingers in action later wrote, "I have seen a stone shot from a sling break a sword in two when it was held in a man's hand thirty yards [27 m] away."[30]

In addition, Aztec warriors employed swords, which were substantially different than Spanish ones. A sword widely used in Mesoamerica, the *maquauhuitl*, for example, consisted of a sturdy wooden handle with thin channels to hold blades. Those blades were made of razor-sharp slices of stone (most often obsidian) rather than the steel used in Spanish swords. The Aztecs used two kinds of *maquauhuitl*—a one-handed variety and a two-handed version. Whereas the one-handed sword was roughly 3 feet (1 m) long, the two-handed one was nearly twice as long. Each *maquauhuitl* looked like a club; on closer inspection, though, one could see the thin blades protruding from its sides.

The weapon shown here is an Aztec atlatl, essentially a throwing stick. One inserted a short spear-like missile in its upper section, tightly gripped the handle, and forcefully flipped the atlatl, sending the missile flying at a high velocity.

One of Cortés's soldiers remembered seeing an Aztec warrior armed with a *maquauhuitl* in the midst of battle. A mounted Spaniard approached the warrior, who swung the stone weapon with amazing force. The blow "struck the horse in the chest," the writer noted, "cutting through to the inside and killing the horse on the spot." That same day, he witnessed "another Indian give a horse a sword thrust in the neck that laid the horse dead at his feet."[31]

"Something Wonderful to See"

The Aztecs' stone weapons made up their primary offensive capability. Their defensive capacity began with their helmets and armor. The helmets were made of wood, animal bone, or bone covered by thick layers of cloth. Also, at least some Aztec soldiers used actual animal skulls as helmets. The body armor these fighters wore consisted most often of sheets of cloth with compressed clumps of raw cotton stuffed between the sheets. Nobles and the most celebrated soldiers often added thick layers of feathers to the outer cloth sheet. The feathers gave a bit of extra protection while also displaying the warrior's high social status.

"[I saw] another Indian give a horse a sword thrust in the neck that laid the horse dead at his feet."[31]

—A Spaniard on the effect of an Aztec stone sword

Fortunately for modern researchers, a vivid description of such a colorful Aztec military array has survived in an anonymous Spaniard's account of his visit to Mexico under Cortés. On the natives' armor, he said, the cloth layers were "the thickness of a finger and a half and sometimes two fingers, which is very strong." Still another cloth layer was added to the others and tied in the back. "These are covered with feathers of different colors, [and] the strength of their feathered garments is proportionate to their weapons, so that they resist spears and arrows, and even the sword. To defend the head, they wear [helmets] of wood, covered on the outside with feathers [or] gold or precious stones, and are something wonderful to see."[32]

Other important defensive tools the Aztecs used were shields, called *yaochimalli* in Nahuatl. Craftsmen fashioned them from wood, animal hides, strips of bamboo, and other materials, sometimes used in various combinations. It was common for soldiers to decorate their shields with paint, feathers, and/or small wood carvings. According to Spaniards and other Europeans who saw Aztec warriors in battle, the shields were highly effective. Native shields "are so strong," one Spaniard remarked, "that only a good crossbow can shoot through them, but arrows [from an ordinary bow] do not damage them."[33]

Confronting the Enemy

With its assortment of defensive and offensive weapons, an Aztec army constituted a formidable-looking and awe-inspiring spectacle. According to a Spanish eyewitness, "It is one of the most beautiful sights in the

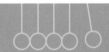

The Aztecs Attack

When an Aztec military leader gave the order for battle to commence, the missile throwers led the way. Evidence indicates that the archers and slingers unleashed their barrage at a distance of roughly 55 to 66 yards (50 to 60 m) from the enemy's front line. The attackers carrying atlatls fired their own weapons from a somewhat closer distance. Then these fighters (called skirmishers in Western military terms) withdrew to make way for the onslaught of the Aztec infantry. Historian Ross Hassig describes the ensuing moments of such a battle:

> The best and most experienced warriors initiated the clash between opposing armies in the hope of delivering the decisive blow. [The generals and other] leaders entered battle at the head of their respective units, which were composed of intermixed veteran and novice warriors so the veterans could support, teach, and watch over the youths in combat. The king usually entered the battle with his entourage of generals [and] order was rigidly maintained in battle. Anyone who broke ranks or caused confusion was beaten or slain, as was anyone who committed any hostility without the order of his leader. Whenever warriors were killed or disabled, the rest closed ranks. [The actual] battlefield tactics varied according to local conditions, opponents, and so forth, but the Aztec army generally tried to surround the enemy and assail it from all sides.

Ross Hassig, *Aztec Warfare: Imperial Expansion and Political Control.* Norman: University of Oklahoma Press, 1988, pp. 99–101.

world to see them in their battle array."[34] Just prior to and during battle, these fighters were organized into units of various sizes. The smallest ones contained twenty men each, and larger groups contained up to four hundred soldiers. The leader of a larger unit customarily hailed from the same town or neighborhood as did the men he commanded.

When an Aztec army confronted an enemy force, the battle most often took place in the early morning hours. The highest-ranking Aztec general—or in some cases the king, if he was present—formed the units into a long line facing the enemy army. At that leader's signal, the long-range missile throwers—that is, the archers and slingers—moved forward and began their deadly barrage. At somewhat closer range, the soldiers carrying atlatls, which had a shorter effective range than other missile weapons, started to unleash their dangerous darts. The overall aim of this collective bombardment was to inflict enough damage to disorient and demoralize the enemy.

When the Aztec leader deemed the time was right, he ordered some men to blow shell trumpets that signaled the infantry charge. A European who saw such a battle recalled that soldiers produced a frightening war cry and surged forward at a run. These foot soldiers crashed into the enemy front line and began employing their shock weapons, including clubs and the lethal stone-bladed swords. At this point, scholar Ross Hassig suggests, "the slingers and archers probably remained back because they were extremely vulnerable to shock-weapon attack, which inflicted the decisive injuries."[35]

Evidence suggests that a Mesoamerican battle of this sort usually lasted at least an hour but could sometimes carry on for two or three times that long. Taking part in furious hand-to-hand combat for so long would be without question extremely tiring. To deal with that reality, an exhausted Aztec soldier withdrew from the battlefield and rested for a while. During that interval, a warrior who had been held in reserve took his place in the fray. Depending on the circumstances, the two might switch places two, three, or more times.

Traditions That Defined War and Society

One goal of the attacking Aztecs was, of course, to kill many enemy fighters. However, it was imperative not to slay all, or even most, of them. This was because a key military and social custom strongly encouraged a soldier to capture one or more members of an opposing army. Put simply, if a warrior could take at least one, and preferably two or more, enemy soldiers prisoner, his military rank and social status would be enhanced.

To ensure that the captives were counted correctly, an Aztec officer known as the master of the captives inspected all prisoners and established exactly who had captured each. This was essential to make certain that no warrior later attempted to inflate his capture record in hopes of reaping more rewards and social honors than he deserved.

Allowing a soldier to garner various gifts and higher social status was not the only motive behind the Aztec custom of taking military prisoners. In addition, the belief was that it was essential to amass a fair number of live captives so that the high priests could sacrifice them to the always bloodthirsty war deity Huitzilopochtli. To that end, Aztec soldiers bound the prisoners and marched them back to Tenochtitlán. There, the captives ascended the many steps of the god's

This illustration is from Spanish friar Diego Durán's 1579 book *The History of the Indies of New Spain*. Duran closely studied Aztec culture, including religious customs such as human sacrifice, graphically depicted in the illustration.

towering pyramid to the temple at its summit, where they endured the horror of having their hearts ripped from their squirming bodies.

Such were the principal military customs that made the Aztecs so successful in their conquests and defined them as a people. Their weapons and strategies, and their belief that their military might made them invincible, endured for generation after generation until 1519. In that fateful year, the Aztecs and other Mesoamericans had to deal with the culture shock that came with finding out that other countries filled with strange peoples existed across the oceans that bordered Mexico. Furthermore, the Spanish newcomers who were among those foreigners had devastating weapons that threatened to turn warfare as the Aztecs knew it on its head. As subsequent events would show, the Aztecs' long era of military confidence and authority was about to end both abruptly and tragically.

CHAPTER FIVE

How Did Foreign Aggression and Greed Destroy the Aztec Civilization?

Focus Questions

1. How did the Aztecs' long-standing dominance lead to their eventual vulnerability and defeat?
2. In your view, if the Spaniards had not found gold in Mexico, would they likely have departed? Why or why not?
3. Could the Aztecs have defeated the Spaniards if they had used different tactics? Explain your answer.

In one of history's most vivid examples of historical cause and effect, in 1519 a small group of Spaniards landed in Mexico and conquered the Aztecs. In fewer than three years, the once mighty realm established by the worshippers of the great god Huitzilopochtli was dismantled. The surviving Aztecs and their Mesoamerican neighbors thereafter had to live under Spanish rule in a land the intruders now called their own.

The invasion and transformation of native Mesoamerica was driven by multiple factors. The Spaniards' desire to get their hands on new and vast amounts of land for exploitation was one factor. Perhaps even more crucial, however, was the Spanish lust for gold and other treasures that the natives were rumored to possess. According to scholar Nicole Schabus, the Spanish conquest of Mexico was in large degree "aimed at the discovery of gold and other natural resources."[36]

Many Spaniards (like numerous other Europeans of that time) demonstrated huge appetites to acquire gold and other riches. When the Aztec king sent the newcomers some gold trinkets in hopes they would be appeased and leave, the gifts had the complete opposite effect. A native account penned later recalled that these "Spaniards burst into smiles. Their eyes shone with pleasure [and] they picked up the gold and fingered it like monkeys. It was as if their hearts were satisfied, brightened, calmed. For in truth they longed and lusted for gold. Their bodies swelled with greed [and] they hungered like pigs for that gold."[37]

Another factor that drove the Spaniards during the conquest of Mexico was their belief in their own racial and religious superiority. Cortés and most of his followers viewed the Aztecs as lowly savages. And, because the latter were not Christians, Cortés saw them as religiously misguided individuals who must be forced to accept what the Spanish viewed as the one true god.

For these reasons, Cortés and other Spanish leaders saw nothing wrong with brutalizing and killing as many natives as it took to establish Spanish control of Mexico. This explains why the invaders committed mass murder, mayhem, and wanton destruction on an almost unprecedented scale. The Aztecs, who were unprepared for and bewildered by the Spaniards' often devious negotiating tactics and outright disregard for nonwhite people, succumbed to near genocide in short order.

Displays of Hospitality and Power

In fact, from the moment the Spaniards landed in eastern Mexico in April 1519, both the Aztec king, Montezuma II, and his people were thrown off guard by a potent case of culture shock. The Aztecs were used to being feared and respected as the most powerful people in the known world. Thus, Spanish treatment of them as inferiors was completely alien to them.

Similarly, Montezuma had long enjoyed immense power, prestige, and respect. He had personally engaged in many conquests and had quelled several rebellions among his realm's subject peoples. By 1519, therefore, he had become a confident ruler who could not conceive of a political or military problem that he could not solve. The arrival of

Cortés and his small army of Spaniards presented the Aztec monarch with new, unprecedented problems with which he ultimately had no effective way of dealing.

The king's initial reports about these strangers' sudden appearance came from some of his subjects who dwelled on the eastern ocean's shores. They sent word that they had seen "two towers or small mountains floating on the waves of the sea." Some men had crawled out of these towers into a small boat and started fishing. After a while, they had climbed back into their towers. "There were about fifteen of these people," the witnesses claimed, "some with blue jackets, others with red, [and] they have very light skin, much lighter than ours. They all have long beards, and their hair comes only to their ears."[38]

It is impossible to know exactly what Montezuma thought about the unexpected arrival of this handful of light-skinned strangers. It seems as if he decided that it would be best to deal with them carefully, in case they might present a threat to his people and empire. To

This is the Mexican artist Juan Ortega's 1885 painting depicting Spaniard Hernán Cortés and his lieutenants meeting the Aztec king Montezuma. Cortés pretended to a be a respectful friend but soon turned on and eventually murdered Montezuma.

that end, he sent messengers bearing gifts to the newcomers. Speaking through Malinche, a Mesoamerican women who spoke Nahuatl and was traveling with and translating for the Spaniards, the messengers told Cortés that their ruler was aware of the strangers' arrival. The great Montezuma had decided to grant them food and shelter, the Aztec envoys explained.

Cortés gladly welcomed this display of hospitality. But he also took advantage of the opportunity to instill some healthy fear in the messengers, realizing that they would convey their alarm to the Aztec king. During the conversation, Cortés ordered his men to fire a few cannons. Instantly, the messengers cowered in terror, and at least one of them fainted.

When the heralds returned to Tenochtitlán, they informed Montezuma of the wonders they had witnessed. About the cannon, they told him that "a thing like a ball of stone comes out of its entrails [guts]." That ball "comes out shooting sparks and raining fire," they added, and "the smoke that comes out with it has a pestilent [deadly] odor, like that of rotten mud." Moreover, "if the cannon is aimed against a mountain, the mountain splits and cracks open. If it is aimed against a tree, it shatters the tree into splinters."[39]

The Spaniards' Bloody Inland March

The messengers also described to Montezuma the newcomers' metal swords and armor and pale skin. The report he had heard surprised and troubled the king. He ordered his spies to closely observe the strangers and their actions in the coming weeks. Montezuma did not yet fully understand that the bearded visitors were from a faraway, well-populated place called Spain. Their leader, Hernán Cortés, had been born in that land in 1484, eighteen years before Montezuma had ascended the Aztec throne.

As a young man Cortés had become a soldier and fought in battles before deciding to seek his fortune in the new Spanish colonies in the Americas. Hoping to become wealthy, he had settled down as a cattle rancher on the large Spanish-ruled island of Cuba. There, he had realized his dream by becoming rich quickly.

Thirsting for still more wealth, as well as adventure, Cortés next used his influence to gain command of an expedition to the then-

Montezuma: A Once-Powerful King

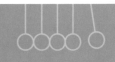

Ever since Montezuma II's death in 1520, descendants of the Aztecs, along with historians and amateur history buffs, have viewed him as a tragic historical figure. He was thirty-four when he became king of the Aztecs in 1502, which made him fifty-one when the Spaniards landed in eastern Mexico in 1519. A contemporary Spanish writer, Bernal Díaz del Castillo, who met Montezuma, described him as tall, on the thin side, muscular, and clean-cut. The king made sure to always wear clean, attractive clothes, Díaz del Castillo stated. Montezuma's considerable power was reflected in the magnificence of the meals he ate, the Spaniard said. Each day the king's cooks provided him with "cooked fowl, turkeys, pheasants, native partridges, quail, tame and wild ducks, venison [deer], wild boar, reed birds, pigeons, hares and rabbits, and many sorts of birds and other things which are bred in this country, and they are so numerous that I cannot finish naming them in a hurry." Another surviving account depicts the authority and respect Montezuma enjoyed among his people. He was quite "skilled in all arts, civil as well as military," it says. "His subjects greatly respected him [and] none of his predecessors, in comparison, could approach his great state and majesty. [In addition] he was so greatly feared by his vassals, and by his captains and leaders, that when they negotiated with him, out of the great esteem and fear that they had, none dared look him in the face."

Bernal Díaz del Castillo, *The Conquest of New Spain*, trans. J.M. Cohen. New York: Penguin, 1963, p. 209.

Quoted in Frances F. Berdan and Patricia R. Anawalt, eds., *Codex Mendoza*, vol. 4. Berkeley: University of California Press, 1992, p. 34.

mysterious Mexican mainland. When he departed Cuba in February 1519, he had eleven ships. They carried 530 Spanish and other European soldiers, a few hundred Cuban Indians and Africans, plus twenty cannons, a few dozen primitive handheld guns known as arquebuses, and sixteen horses.

With this small but powerful military ensemble, Cortés moved inland from the eastern Mexican coast with the goal of reaching the Aztec capital of Tenochtitlán. Surely, he reasoned, it would hold vast amounts of gold and other valuable materials. A native description of the Spaniards' march has survived, explaining that the newcomers "came raising dust. Their iron lances seemed to glisten." Also, some Spaniards were dressed "all in iron." Those fantastic foreigners "came gleaming, hence they [marched along] causing great astonishment. Hence they [marched] causing great fear."[40]

On September 23, 1519, the Spaniards reached the valley of Tlaxcala. The only local people whom the Aztecs had not yet defeated, the Tlaxcalans despised the residents of Tenochtitlán and their ruler. Hearing this, Cortés was delighted and offered to form a pact between his forces and these local Indians. The Tlaxcalan king agreed to the deal on the condition that the Spaniards would help him defeat another Tlaxcalan enemy, the Cholulans, who dwelled several miles to the south. Anxious to acquire the Tlaxcalan as allies, as well as to do some plundering, Cortés agreed. Swiftly he led his forces southward and, in an audacious, bloody assault on Cholula, mercilessly massacred thousands of its inhabitants.

Montezuma Meets Cortés

After this violent event, the Spaniards pressed on toward Tenochtitlán. They arrived at Lake Texcoco on November 8. At the sight of the magnificent city in the distance, Cortés and his followers were astounded by its enormous size and grandeur. One of those Spaniards later recalled, "The circumference of this city is from two and a half to three leagues [8 miles, or 13 kilometers]. Most of the persons who have seen it judge it to have sixty thousand inhabitants or more. [The city] has many beautiful and wide streets [and] very beautiful squares [and] many beautiful houses belonging to the [Aztec] lords."[41]

To reach the city's entrance, the awed visitors had to march along a sturdily constructed stone causeway 5 miles (8 km) long. Approaching the capital's main gates, they saw that thousands of people had gathered on nearby rooftops. Clearly, those natives hoped to witness firsthand these bizarre travelers from a distant country whom they had heard so much about.

Montezuma initially ordered his people to offer no resistance to the foreigners. After a little while, wearing a splendid outfit, he exited the gates and approached the waiting Spaniards. The king walked to Cortés and placed a golden necklace around his neck. Cortés smiled and hung a handsome string of painted beads around Montezuma's neck. With Malinche dutifully translating, the Spanish commander queried, "Are you Montezuma? Are you the king?" Montezuma replied, "Yes, I am Montezuma." To Malinche, Cortés said, "Tell Montezuma that we are his friends. There is nothing to fear. We have wanted to see him for a long time, and now we have seen his face and heard his words. Tell him that we love him well and that our hearts are contented."[42]

> "Tell Montezuma that we are his friends. There is nothing to fear."[42]
>
> —Cortés to the translator in a dialogue with the Aztec king

Betrayal, Plunder, and Mass Murder

This talk of friendship between the two leaders was short-lived, in large part because of Cortés's duplicity. He and his followers were fully aware that they had come to loot the natives and rob them of their land. With these goals in mind, once the Spaniards had entered Tenochtitlán without a fight, they did not waste much time pretending to be friends.

In fact, only eight days after his arrival in the city, Cortés ordered Montezuma's arrest. At first most Aztecs did not realize what had happened. In private, Cortés used dire threats to control the king, force him to act as if nothing had happened, and to pretend to go on ruling the city. In reality, however, the Spaniard was now giving the orders in the capital.

Meanwhile, Cortés and his officers repeatedly grilled Montezuma, demanding that he tell them where his royal valuables were kept. Naively assuming that if he complied the intruders would go away, the king revealed the locations of his treasure troves. Arriving at one such storage facility, a native account states, the Spaniards "searched everywhere." Acting as if they had entered the heavens where the gods dwelled, the account continues, "they were slaves to their own greed. All of Montezuma's possessions were brought out." The looters "seized these treasures as if they were their own, as if this plunder was merely a stroke of good luck. And when they had taken all the gold, they heaped up everything else in the middle of the patio."[43]

Even after this outrage, Montezuma failed to recognize that the Spaniards were only getting started. The king likely figured that sooner or later his people would catch on and kill the interlopers. After all, Cortés had only a few hundred men, but Montezuma had thousands of warriors. The threats posed by the Spaniards' cannons and their many native allies were evidently not yet apparent to the Aztec monarch.

Thereafter, a series of violent events occurred in fairly rapidly succession. In April 1520 Cortés departed to take care of some of-

Depicted here is the horrifying moment when Cortés's assistant, Pedro de Alvarado, ordered a sneak attack on hundreds of unsuspecting Aztecs in the midst of prayer. Other locals retaliated and trapped the Spaniards in the royal palace.

Sadly Contrasting Views of Gold

History is filled with moments of irony, situations in which something oc-curs in a manner contrary to how people would expect it to happen. Often people see in such ironies either humor or sadness. Here, scholar Stuart Matthews points out both humor and sadness in the contrast between how the Spaniards who invaded Mexico viewed gold and how the Aztecs saw that yellow-colored metal.

> The tragic irony to the gold-thirsty Spanish missions to the New World is that prior to their arrival gold was not particularly precious to the Meso-americans. The Aztecs had no metallic currency and used gold and sil-ver only for ceremonial and personal decoration. In fact, due to an over-abundance of gold, the Aztecs referred to it as "the excrement [poop] of the gods," eagerly trading their substantial supplies of the "excrement" in the feathers and turquoise markets. This is perhaps humorously tell-ing as to why the Aztec leader Montezuma first offered the Spaniards gold in an attempt to get them to leave his land, rather than the feather and turquoise commodities that carried higher Aztec market value. However, Montezuma was not aware of the European mercantilist [fi-nancial] system that bestowed upon gold more value than any other natural resource. Rather than invoking a retreat from Mexico, the gifts of gold only served to whet the Spanish appetite for extreme wealth.

Stuart Matthews, "Cortés and Aztec Gold: International Conflict and Modern Political Ecol-ogy," *ICE Case Studies*, no. 174, March 2006, American University. www1.american.edu.

ficial Spanish business on the coast and left his officer Pedro de Alvarado in charge of Tenochtitlán. Alvarado may have wanted to show the locals that he was boss. Or perhaps as a devout Christian he intended to teach them that their faith was false. Whatever his motivations were, he ordered his soldiers to launch a sneak attack on thousands of unarmed men and women who were in the midst of worship. A surviving account says that the Spanish soldiers "attacked all the celebrants, stabbing them, spearing them, striking them with their swords." The soldiers beheaded others or "split their heads to pieces." Some Aztecs tried to escape but could not. Blood "flowed like water and gathered into pools, [and] the stench of blood and entrails filled the air."[44]

When Cortés returned a few days later, he was shocked to find that the city's residents—women and men alike—had struck back. They had attacked the Spaniards and trapped them inside Montezuma's palace. Cortés told the king to order his irate people to fall back. But the Aztecs now viewed their ruler as a pawn of the intruders, so they refused to listen to his pleas. At this point, seeing Montezuma as no longer useful to him, Cortés had him, along with all of the Aztec nobles in the palace, strangled to death.

The Broken Spears

This turned out to be a colossal mistake. The Aztecs viewed these vicious murders as the final outrage. In July 1520 they attacked the Spaniards in force, chasing them along one of the stone causeways that crossed the lake. In a furious battle, more than six hundred Spaniards and their allies were slain. Many of them died because the large bags of treasure they were lugging slowed them down.

Cortés and some of his followers managed to escape from the carnage of what Spanish writers later came to call the Noche Triste, or "Night of Sorrows." The Aztecs celebrated their victory and chose a new king, named Cuitláhuac, who assumed the Spaniards would cause his people no further harm. But he was wrong.

Not only did Cortés vow to return, he and his men had left behind another army, an invisible one made up of germs. The Spaniards were unaware that they had brought smallpox with them from Europe. The natives, who had no natural resistance to the disease, as the Spaniards did, soon started dying by the thousands.

The plague horribly decimated the Aztecs. When Cortés returned five months later with Spanish reinforcements from Cuba, plus tens of thousands of native allies, he found Tenochtitlán's defenders badly weakened. During the ensuing siege the Aztecs courageously resisted

Cortés (on the horse at center) enters the Tlaxcalan capital to meet with his ally, the local king, in preparation for the impending final siege of the Aztec city of Tenochtitlan.

for an amazing eighty days, but their sad fate was never in question. On August 13, 1521, Cortés achieved his final victory

When Tenochtitlán fell, the Aztec empire simply ceased to exist. Some Aztecs survived. Yet they, along with most other Mesoamericans, became slaves or servants to droves of incoming Spanish settlers who swiftly transformed Mexico into the Spanish colony of New Spain. Reflecting on how foreign arrogance and greed had destroyed his homeland, a despondent Aztec poet summed up the prevailing feelings of the natives. "Broken spears lie in the roads," he wrote. "We have torn our hair in grief. The houses are roofless now, and their walls are red with blood." Everywhere, he said, there was utter despair, "for our inheritance, our city, is lost and dead." Sorrowfully he added, "Know that with these disasters we have lost the Mexican nation."[45]

Introduction: The Heart of a Toltec

1. Michael E. Smith, *The Aztecs*. Oxford, UK: Blackwell, 2002, p. 37.
2. Lewis Spence, "Mexican Mythology: Tezcatlipoca and the Toltecs." www.sacred-texts.com.
3. Mark Cartwright, "Toltec Civilization," *Ancient History Encyclopedia*. www.ancient.eu.

Chapter One: A Brief History of Aztec Civilization

4. Frances F. Berdan, *The Aztecs of Central Mexico: An Imperial Society*. Belmont, CA: Wadsworth, 2004, p. 2.
5. Duncan Ryan, *The Aztec: The Last Great Civilization of Mesoamerica*. Charleston, SC: Amazon Digital, 2016, p. 3.
6. Berdan, *Aztecs of Central Mexico*, pp. 3, 6.
7. Brian M. Fagan, *Kingdoms of Gold, Kingdoms of Jade: The Americas Before Columbus*. New York: Thames and Hudson, 1991, p. 23.
8. Warwick Bray, *Everyday Life of the Aztecs*. London: B.T. Batsford, 1991, p. 116.
9. Fagan, *Kingdoms of Gold, Kingdoms of Jade*, p. 33.
10. Quoted in John P. Schmal, "The Rise of the Aztec Empire," Houston Institute for Culture. www.houstonculture.org.
11. Edward Lawler, "Central and South American Empires, Part 2." www.ushistory.org.
12. Quoted in Miguel León-Portilla, *Pre-Columbian Literatures of Mexico*. Norman: University of Oklahoma Press, 1969, p. 87.

Chapter Two: How Did Religion Spur the Aztec Migration into Mexico?

13. Guilhem Olivier, "The Gods of the Mexica, Part 2," Mexicolore. www.mexicolore.co.uk.
14. Olivier, "The Gods of the Mexica, Part 2."
15. Smith, *The Aztecs*, p. 211.
16. Quoted in Diego Durán, *The History of the Indies of New Spain*, trans. Doris Heyden. Norman: University of Oklahoma Press, 1994, pp. 43–44.
17. Quoted in Durán, *The History of the Indies of New Spain*, p. 44.

Chapter Three: How Did Reverence for the Gods Shape the Aztecs' Creative Expression?

18. Eduardo M. Moctezuma, "Aztec History and Cosmovision," in *Moctezuma's Mexico: Visions of the Aztec World*, by David Carrasco and Eduardo M. Moctezuma. Niwot: University Press of Colorado, 1992, p. 41.
19. Julia Flood, "Were the Aztecs as Barbaric as Described by the Spanish?," Mexicolore. www.mexicolore.co.uk.
20. Jaime Cóttrill, "Ancient Aztec Art." www.aztec-history.com.
21. Cóttrill, "Ancient Aztec Art."
22. Manuel Aguilar-Moreno, *Handbook to Life in the Aztec World*. New York: Oxford University Press, 2006, p. 222.
23. Moctezuma, "Aztec History and Cosmovision," p. 66.
24. Jaime Cóttrill, "Aztec Masks." www.aztec-history.com.
25. Daniel G. Brinton, trans., "Hymn of Huitzilopochtli," Internet Sacred Text Archive. www.sacred-texts.com.

Chapter Four: How Did Warfare Define the Aztecs' Identity and Success as a People?

26. Aguilar-Moreno, *Handbook to Life in the Aztec World*, p. 98.
27. Diego Durán, *Book of the Gods and Rites and the Aztec Calendar*, trans. Fernando Horcasites and Doris Heyden. Norman: University of Oklahoma Press, 1971, p. 197.
28. Durán, *The History of the Indies of New Spain*, p. 554.
29. Garcilaso de la Vega, *The Florida of the Inca*, trans. John and Jeannette Varner. Austin: University of Texas Press, 1951, p. 597.
30. Alonzo Enriquez de Guzman, *The Life and Acts of Don Alonzo Enriquez de Guzman, Knight of Seville*, trans. Clements R. Markham. London: Hakluyt Society, 1862, p. 99.
31. Quoted in Patricia de Fuentes, ed., *The Conquistadors: First-Person Accounts of the Conquest of Mexico*. Norman: University of Oklahoma Press, 1993, p. 169.
32. Quoted in Fuentes, *The Conquistadors*, pp. 168–69.
33. Quoted in Fuentes, *The Conquistadors*, p. 169.
34. Quoted in Ross Hassig, *Aztec Warfare: Imperial Expansion and Political Control*. Norman: University of Oklahoma Press, 1988, p. 124.
35. Hassig, *Aztec Warfare*, p. 99.

Chapter Five: How Did Foreign Aggression and Greed Destroy the Aztec Civilization?

36. Nicole Schabus, "No Power to International Trade with Indigenous Property," *Journal for Developmental Policy,* vol. 18, 2002, p. 99.

37. Quoted in Miguel León-Portilla, ed., *The Broken Spears: The Aztec Account of the Conquest of Mexico.* Boston: Beacon, 2011, p. 51.

38. Quoted in León-Portilla, *The Broken Spears,* pp. 16–17.

39. Quoted in León-Portilla, *The Broken Spears,* p. 39.

40. Bernardino de Sahagún, *Florentine Codex: General History of the Things of New Spain,* vol. 12, trans. J.O. Anderson and Charles E. Dibble. Santa Fe, NM: School of American Research and University of Utah, 1950, p. 39.

41. Quoted in Fuentes, *The Conquistadors,* p. 146.

42. Quoted in León-Portilla, *The Broken Spears,* pp. 64–65.

43. Quoted in León-Portilla, *The Broken Spears,* pp. 68–69.

44. Quoted in León-Portilla, *The Broken Spears,* pp. 74, 76.

45. Quoted in León-Portilla, *The Broken Spears,* pp. 137–39.

FOR FURTHER RESEARCH

Books

Irwin R. Blacker, *Cortés and the Aztec Conquest*. Charleston, SC: CreateSpace, 2016.

Hourly History, *Aztecs: A History from Beginning to End*. New York: Hourly History, 2016.

Natalie Hyde, *Understanding Mesoamerican Myths*. New York: Crabtree, 2013.

Miguel León-Portilla, ed., *The Broken Spears: The Aztec Account of the Conquest of Mexico*. Boston: Beacon, 2007.

Charles Phillips, *The Complete Illustrated History of the Aztec and Maya*. London: Hermes House, 2015.

Internet Sources

"The Aztec Gods—Who's Who" (www.aztec.history.com/aztec-history.com/aztec-gods.html.) On this useful webpage, a Mexican scholar tells about five of the leading Aztec gods.

"Aztec Origins and the Founding of Tenochtitlan" (http://archaeology.about.com/od/aztecarchaeology/a/aztec_origins.htm). This About .com overview of the supposed origins of the Aztecs tells how they journeyed from somewhere far to the north and established their capital city in the Valley of Mexico.

Conquistadors (www.pbs.org/conquistadors/index.html). PBS produced this fact-filled documentary about the Spanish soldiers who conquered the Aztecs.

"How the Aztecs Discovered Corn" (www.mexicolore.co.uk/aztecs/stories/discovery-of-corn). As shown in this article by Julia Flood, the Aztecs had a colorful myth about how they were introduced to one of their staple foods.

"Quetzalcoatl" (www.mythencyclopedia.com/Pr-Sa/Quetzalcoatl.html). The online *Myths Encyclopedia* provides this fairly detailed synopsis of the legendary ancient Aztec ruler who was said to have sailed away over the eastern horizon.

Cover: Close-up of a mural on the wall, Quetzalcoatl Gives Indians The Gift Of Maize, Palace Of The Governor, Tlaxcala, Mexico/De Agostini Picture Library/G. Dagli Orti/ Bridgeman Images

6: lucidwaters/Depositphotos.com (top); Diego Grandi/Shutterstock.com (bottom);

7: Juan Aunion/Shutterstock.com (top); Photos.com/Thinkstock.com (bottom)

9: A bustling marketplace in the Aztec capital of Tenochtitlan, 1987 (colour litho), Hall, H. Tom (1932–2010)/National Geographic Creative/Bridgeman Images

15: Manuscript, Mexico, 16th century. Construction of the city of Tenochtitlan, Aztecs strengthening the land using chinampas method. Copy/De Agostini Picture Library/G. Dagli Orti/Bridgeman Images

19: Partial cross-section of the Great Temple at Tenochtitlan (w/c on paper), French School, (20th century)/Archives Larousse, Paris, France/Bridgeman Images

21: Maury Aaseng

26: Priest offering the heart taken from a living human victim to the Aztec sun god and god of war, Huitzilopochtli. Print of facsimile from Aztec Codex, published 1904. Human Sacrifice/Universal History Archive/UIG/Bridgeman Images

29: Types of Pre-Colombian constructions in Tenochtitlan, Mexico. Aztec Civilization, 14th–16th Century/De Agostini Picture Library/G. Dagli Orti/Bridgeman Images

32: Mexico, 14th century—according to the prophecy, the Aztecs founded Tenochtitlan in 1325, in the place where an eagle devours a snake perched on a cactus (oil on wood), Mexican School/Museo de la Ciudad, Mexico/De Agostini Picture Library/A. Dagli Orti/Bridgeman Images

37: Sun Stone or Aztec Calendar Stone, found in Tenochtitlan in 1789, Mexico, Azteca Civilization, 15th century/De Agostini Picture Library/G. Sioen/Bridgeman Images

39: Urn depicting Tlaloc, rain god, polychrome ceramic, height 35 cm, from Tomb No 21 at Templo Mayor, Tenochtitlan, Mexico, Aztec civilization, 15th century/Museo del Templo Mayor, Mexico City, Mexico/De Agostini Picture Library/G. Dagli Orti/Bridgeman Images

44: Facsimile copy of codex Borbonicus, detail depicting the elaboration of the Oxomoco and Cipactonal calendar (vellum), Aztec/Private Collection/Jean-Pierre Courau/Bridgeman Images

49: Guido Sansoni Mondadori Portfolio/Newscom

53: Gold leaf on wood javelin thrower (atlatl), recto. Aztec civilization, Mexico/De Agostini Picture Library/G. Dagli Orti/Bridgeman Images

57: Miniature depicting human sacrifice, from Mexican manuscript entitled The History of the Indies of New Spain by Diego Duran, 1579/De Agostini Picture Library/G. Dagli Orti/Bridgeman Images

61: Hernan Cortes meeting Montezuma, painting by Juan Ortega, 1885, Mexico, 16th century/De Agostini Picture Library/G. Dagli Orti/Bridgeman Images

66: Pedro de Alvarado and his soldiers massacring the Aztecs, c.1520 (engraving), Bry, Theodore de (1528–98)/John Judkyn Memorial, Bath, Avon, UK/Bridgeman Images

69: Entrance of the Triumphant Army of Cortes into Tlaxcala after the Victory of Otumba, 19th century (oil on panel), Spanish School, (19th century)/Museo de America, Madrid, Spain/Index/Bridgeman Images

Historian and award-winning author Don Nardo has written numerous books about Native American peoples and their histories and cultures, including volumes on the precontact Native Americans, Mesoamerican myths, the North American Indian wars, Native American weapons, US Indian removal and relocation policies, and photographer Edward S. Curtis's work with Indian cultures. Nardo, who also composes and arranges orchestral music, lives with his wife, Christine, in Massachusetts.